Contents

Contents _____

For more than twenty-five years Alastair Lockhart has been selling innovative social stationery at his shop in Walton Street, London SW3. Five years ago he changed the emphasis completely and now concentrates exclusively on custom designed and printed orders. These are Wedding & Party Invitations, Writing paper & Correspondence cards, Birth Announcement, Visiting cards, Change of Address cards, in fact almost everything you personally might need.

The shop boasts probably the best and most comprehensive selection of designs for wedding invitations you will find in London. As well as the Crane and William Arthur collections from America and the beautiful calligraphy of Pendragon Ink with its individually hand-painted flowers, the company will design invitations especially for you using its in-house facilities and British printers. There are books, portfolios of designs and examples to look through for all kinds of celebrations. There is a comprehensive selection of papers and boards in different tints, textures and weights from suppliers all round the world.

A typical wedding invitation package would include the Invitation, Reply cards and envelopes, Order-of-Service sheets, Thank-you cards and perhaps Menus and Place cards. For international weddings, in addition to the usual items, there will be a full itinerary of events and information of what to expect and what to wear. If you are planning a weekend by the Bosphorus, a masked ball in Venice, a few days in Provence or tying the knot on top of a mountain in Switzerland, you will need plenty of guidance.

When asked ìWhat have you got that is different in Wedding Invitations?î the truthful answer is ìHow far will your imagination allow you to go?î In our multi-cultural, international society, the more traditional Christian English wedding format is just one of several ways in which we celebrate such an important event. Planning the wedding involves the whole family. Everybody, it would seem, must have his or her say. Alastair Lockhart will often suggest all parties come together to discuss the details particularly when foreign languages are involved. This can help to concentrate the mind on essential details. Discussions are always lively with occasional tears of frustration and misunderstanding but it generally works out successfully in the end. When weddings are not in a house of worship, the wording, decoration, colour, ribbons, etc. becomes important. Getting it wrong can be embarrassing and Alastair Lockhart believes that providing advice is as important as the finished design. The staff at Alastair Lockhart has wide experience of the finer points of etiquette that can arise. Arabic and Farsi calligraphy, Cyrillic, Japanese, Oriental texts and European languages do not present problems. American, though nominally an English language, is managed without hesitation although American etiquette often adheres strictly to the carefully worded guidelines of Amy Vanderbilt or Crane.

When it comes to making the best possible wedding invitations, there is none finer than hand-engraved invitations in copperplate script, carefully printed on a superb smooth white board, heavy enough to stand proudly upright above any fireplace. Alastair Lockhart engraves and prints these here in England and the finished, understated card meet all these requirements perfectly.

Alastair Lockhart produces much of the work in the USA. He believes that the quality of work there is excellent and that generally the printers are quick, dependable and efficient for both engraved and thermographic work. He likes the detailed attention paid to the expectations of the customer of service and presentation. Costs are generally well below similar work in the UK and when courier, duties and taxes are added, still makes for a competitive price in London. The design and typesetting is done at the shop and when the job is complete, shipped by courier to wherever in the world the customer decides.

In a perfect world there would be time enough to complete all the wedding arrangements punctually and in the correct order but it is not. Ordering the invitation should be one of the earliest jobs undertaken. To avoid disappointment and to ensure the best result, it is wise to leave as much time as possible. Even with the arrival of the computer, printing is still a craft business depending on the skills of experienced craftsmen and women, who have spent a lifetime perfecting their work. The process takes time. Nevertheless overall completion times can be as short as a week, and depending on the complexity, generally invitations are finished within three or four weeks.

Most invitations are printed by any one or combination of the normal processes - intaglio or engraving, silkscreen, letterpress, lithography, letterpress and thermography - digital printing is now becoming commonplace. The advantage of this process is that 4-colour work is possible for very short runs at prices within really all budgets.

Everyone at Alastair Lockhart is ready to help create that special invitation for you, to turn your blue skies, dreams and imagination into reality. This is what the company likes to do and what they feel they are best at doing. A visit to the shop will whet your appetite and then you will want to make an appointment to start the grand design.

The company does not have a list of prices, as each job is invariably different. It helps to have worked out beforehand some rough basic information such as dates, numbers of guests and format and extent of the celebrations, all of which can be altered at a later date. This helps to determine the most sensible method of production to meet anticipated completion dates and to estimate the cost.

The shop is open everyday Monday to Friday, 10.00 a.m. to 6.00 p.m. and Saturdays, except 17 July through August 31, from 10.00 a.m. to 5.00 p.m. The shop is closed on Sundays and Bank Holidays and the Millennium Week.

The finest

Wedding Invitations

in the world!

Bride & Groom

W E D D I N G   S E R V I C E

For your *FREE*, full-colour mail order catalogue,
Ring FREEPHONE

0500 006573 or 01506 265002

or write to:
Bride & Groom Wedding Service
Great Central Road,
Loughborough LE11 1RW

or

Request your FREE catalogue on the Internet:
www.Wedding.Order.com

A GUIDE TO GETTING MARRIED

When organising your Wedding Stationary it is important to select the correct invitations which will co-ordinate with the style of your wedding. The look of stationery will set the style of your wedding and will tell people what type of person you are.

Making the choice can prove very difficult as there are so many designs to choose from in the market today. Bride & Groom Wedding Service is a mail order catalogue which allows you to sit in the comfort of your own home to make that important decision. Our catalogue offers a wide range of stationery to suit all tastes from cute, traditional to contemporary all at a price that is affordable.

We offer a wide variety of ink colours for added style and elegance, along with a range of type/styles and wording choices. All invitations have matching order of service, menus, reply cards, thank you cards to allow you to coordinate your stationery.

To add that finishing touch to your day we also offer a wide range of accessories that can be personalised with your names and wedding date if requested. The range includes: Personalised serviettes, cakes boxes match books, personalised champagne flutes, guest books and so much more.

Bride and Groom Wedding Service is the UKs leading Mail Order Wedding Stationery Catalogue. We pride ourselves on producing high quality products and offer a fast efficient delivery service. We have a team of highly trained customer service staff who are available to provide information and advise on all products to make ordering easy and to ensure that you make the right decision.

Bride & Groom Wedding Service offers a 30 day money back guarantee with every item shown in our catalogue. If you are unsatisfied with any product purchased from us, simply return it postage paid within 30 days of receipt for a full refund.

*Should you require further information on our products or would like to request our **FREE 72 page full colour brochure** please contact us on our Freephone number: 0500 006573 where someone will be happy to assist you.*

1 *From I Will to I Do*

When, where and how we marry has changed in recent decades. Fewer of us are tying the knot than ever before, we are marrying later in life, less likely to wed in a religious ceremony and increasing numbers of us are marrying for the second or even third time.

Six in 10 now marry in civil ceremonies and fewer than 4 in 10 in religious services. And of the more than 300,000 couples who will wed this year, only 185,000 will be marrying for the first time. Two-fifths will be a remarriage.

Compare this to the weddings of the last generation and there has been a dramatic change. The number of marriages solemnized by a religious ceremony fell by 36 per cent between 1981 and 1996. In the same year at the start of the 1980s, 65 per cent of all marriages were first-time weddings compared to 58 per cent in 1996.

However, while the institution of marriage may be far different today than it has been in past decades, one aspect of weddings has not altered. Your wedding day will still be one of – if not *the* – most important days of your life. You will want to it be special, memorable, romantic and problem free.

The only way to ensure this is by careful planning. The *Daily Telegraph Guide to Getting Married* is designed to help you prepare for your big day. It should take some of the stress out of organizing the wedding ceremony and celebrations by helping you to plan ahead, taking you step by step through the practical preparations and even helping you with the etiquette of invitations, wedding lists and seating plans.

With the average wedding now costing more than £11,000 according to *Wedding and Home* magazine, planning your finances cannot be ignored. Another tradition that is in decline is for the bride's parents to pay for the entire cost of the wedding. Today it is increasingly common for the bride and groom to contribute financially and in half of all cases they foot the entire party bill.

Then there are the legal and religious implications of a wedding to prepare for. Does the wife take her husband's name? Should you have a joint bank account? What if you do not share the same faith?

There are so many things to think about and so many skills needed – you almost have to become an expert in floristry, catering, event management, printing, dress design and photography just to organize a wedding.

As many brides-to-be and their partners start planning the big day up to 18 months in advance, the whole process can also be long and stressful. And then, of course, there is the day itself to worry about. Will it rain? Will the photographer turn up? What if I have forgotten to book something?

We hope that the *Daily Telegraph Guide to Getting Married* will take some of the stress out of the weeks and months when you are planning your wedding and that it will also give you some practical ideas for making your big day even more memorable.

2 *The Engagement*

As we approach the millennium, tradition is holding fast. The majority of proposals are still made by men and the majority of couples still have a period of engagement before getting married – although the length of engagements has fallen to around 14 months compared to 19 months a decade ago, according to *Wedding and Home* magazine.

The length of an engagement partly depends on the type of wedding you are having. You will generally need to leave at least six months to plan a traditional wedding, whereas a registry office ceremony can be arranged only weeks in advance.

There are other factors involved. An engagement is a useful period to decide whether you are right for each other. So make your engagement period long enough to consider your decision before you wed. It is much easier to break off an engagement than to decide you are not made for each other when it is too late and you are already married.

The Proposal

Although it is still men who do most of the asking, women are increasingly popping the question themselves. Of course, many still wait for 29 February, the traditional day for women to ask for their lover's hand in marriage.

If you are thinking of proposing, you could plan a memorable setting to pop the question. Perhaps choose somewhere of particular significance to you as a couple or just a romantic place like on a bridge at night, in a restaurant or even on an aeroplane as you jet off for a holiday.

Asking for Permission to Wed

The days when asking a father's permission to wed his daughter before proposing to the bride-to-be are long gone. Most brides-to-be today would expect to be consulted first!

However, the tradition does still exist in some sense. It is customary for the hopeful groom to speak to his fiancée's father after he has proposed. This courtesy is an ideal time for the groom to discuss his future intentions and even to reassure the bride's parents about his love for their daughter and confirm that as a couple they are serious about making such a commitment. Even if you are a mature couple or it's a second marriage, it's still a good idea to pay this respect to your future father-in-law and start off on a good foot.

Engagement Announcements

The bride's and groom's parents should be told first and then close family and friends. Usually the bride's mother will contact the bride's relations and family friends while the groom contacts his own relations and friends.

A publication can then be placed in the local and/or national press, by which time, if you know the date of the wedding, it should be recorded in the announcement. It is customary for the bride's parents to pay for an announcement in the national press, while any costs for announcements in the local press are usually footed by the groom or his family. Think about costs and ask for the price of each word. A formal notice of engagement will usually look something like this:

Mr J Nettles and Miss J Jones
The engagement is announced between John Nettles, youngest
son of Mr and Mrs Tom Nettles, Fordingbridge, Hampshire and
Juliet Jones, only daughter of Mr James Jones and Mrs Catherine
Jones of Bristol.

Many couples throw a party to celebrate their engagement with family and friends. This could be an opportunity for the bride's and groom's parents to meet, although it might be better to do this at a more private occasion. A good tip is to keep a note of any presents and whom they came from just in case anything goes wrong and you need to return them!

Meeting the In-laws

If engagement etiquette is followed, it is normal for the parents of the groom-to-be to write to the bride's parents and suggest a date for a meeting. This should be a relaxed social occasion like a lunch or dinner, hosted by the parents of the groom-to-be.

The Engagement Ring

By the time the engagement is announced it is traditional for the engagement ring already to have been bought. As opposed to the wedding ring, the engagement ring commonly has a gemstone. A diamond solitaire is the most popular form. When buying a diamond, keep in mind the four 'C's. The cost of a diamond depends on its 'cut' (how well it has been cut to shape), 'carat' (weight), clarity (how pure or flawless it is) and its colour (the best colour is no colour). If you're using gold for the band, the carat measures quality. Pure gold is 24 carat; for jewellery this is too soft, so 22 carat is the purest form for jewellery.

The band does not have to be made of gold. Don't immediately run to a jewellers; you could find the perfect ring in an antique shop or even in the attic! A family heirloom might be just the thing. The engagement ring should not be of a harder or softer metal than the wedding ring. Over time a platinum ring could wear down a gold one.

Although diamond is the most common choice for an engagement ring, a symbol of strength and security, many couples now opt for a different gemstone. This is particularly the case if a couple have decided not to have an engagement and are buying a wedding and engagement ring in one. You might want to consider birthstones when choosing an alternative gemstone:

January	garnet
February	amethyst
March	aquamarine
April	diamond
May	emerald
June	pearl
July	ruby
August	peridot
September	sapphire
October	opal
November	topaz
December	turquoise

Breaking It Off

An engagement is not legally binding and the former fiancée is under no legal obligation to give the engagement ring back. It is, however, the decent thing to do, especially if she has broken off the engagement.

Most couples have the jitters at one time or another during their wedding preparations, but serious doubts should be listened to and acted upon. If you are breaking off an engagement, the best thing to do is to contact friends and relatives and inform them with as little fuss as possible.

A formal announcement in a newspaper is formal etiquette if you originally announced the engagement in this manner (although you may find this too embarrassing). A formal cancellation will only state the names of the couple and the fact that the wedding will no longer take place. There is no need to give any reasons as to why the engagement has been broken off.

If you had an engagement party, all gifts should be sent back to their individual bearers. If wedding invitations have already been sent out, a formal card should be sent to each of the guests. The announcement could take the following format:

Mr and Mrs Harry Jones announce that the marriage of their daughter, Sophie Anne to Mr Simon Charles Green, which was arranged for Saturday 24 February will not take place.

The Biggest Decision of Your Life

The average age for first marriages is 27 for women and 29 for men – several years older than in 1996.

This increased maturity – and the fact that more of us cohabit before committing to marriage – should mean that we are more prepared.Yet when we do decide to get married, how many of us know what we are really letting ourselves in for? Remember marriage goes on – hopefully – long after the honeymoon.

Couples have to be fully aware of all the changes that taking this huge step entails. Getting married is not just about a big day, a wonderfully expensive frock, an exotic honeymoon and stockpiling wedding gifts in a new home – it is about a commitment to staying together and dealing with life's challenges in turn.

Some people give up all effort at making their relationship work, as if a marriage licence is some magic glue that will bind two people together no matter what. Then there are legal and financial responsibilities that your new status entails.

In this country two out of five marriages end in divorce. This is the highest in Western Europe.

A Time for Reflection

What can be done to prevent this happening? The organization Relate has been running marriage preparation courses since the 1930s. The course is now called Couples and is open to anyone getting married, although usually it is at the suggestion of the vicar marrying a couple. The pair attend three core sessions of up to one hour. They then choose to attend optional sessions on a range of subjects, including money, children, parenting and sex. Each session costs £20 per person. Some couples choose to take these sessions over a weekend. It is open to those who opt to live together or make any form of commitment to one another, too.

The main purpose is to show couples how best to communicate with one another, with the main aim being avoiding conflict and understanding the different stages a relationship goes through. It covers tips on how to decide who does housework, adapting to having children and understanding the issues involved in making a commitment. The ultimate goal is to prevent couples getting to the stage where they require counselling for breakdown of their relationship.

Currently, about 1,000 couples take the course each year. The classes are available from Relate centres around England, Wales and Northern Ireland. Contact Relate on 01788 573241 for more details.

3 The Legal Requirements

Marriage is a legally binding agreement. So before making any of your wedding plans you should at least be aware of what the law requires you to do.

The basic legal requirements are that:

▌ you must give notice of your marriage;

▌ a Superintendent Registrar or authorized person must be present;

▌ you must have two competent witnesses to sign the marriage register;

▌ you must marry between 8 am and 6 pm (unless it's in Scotland or a Jewish or Quaker ceremony).

Where Can You Marry?

You can marry in a Register office, Church of England, Church in Wales, Church of Scotland, Church of Ireland or Roman Catholic Church. If both partners are Jewish you can wed in a synagogue or a private place. Thanks to the 1994 Marriage Act you can tie the knot anywhere that has been approved by your local authority. If you've set your heart on a particular building or beauty spot and want to know if it's possible to get married there, get in touch with the

Superintendent Registrar in the register office covering that area, or you could contact the General Register Office on 0151 471 4200.

Civil Weddings
General Register Office for England and Wales: 0151 471 4200
General Register Office for Scotland: 0131 334 0380
General Register Office for Northern Ireland: 01232 250000
General Register Office for Guernsey: 01481 725 277
Superintendent Registrar for Jersey: 01534 502335

Church Weddings
Church of England Enquiry Centre: 0171 898 1000
Marriage Care (formerly Catholic Marriage Advisory Council): 0171 243 1898
Episcopal Church of Scotland: 0131 225 6537
Greek Orthodox Church Information: 0171 723 4787
Jewish Marriage Council: 0181 203 6311
Methodist Press and Information Centre: 0171 486 5502
Muslim Information Centre: 0171 272 5170
The Hindu Society: 0181 944 0251
United Reformed Church: 0171 916 2020

If you are marrying overseas, where you marry will be dictated by the laws of the country you are marrying in. Contact the country's embassy for further details. If one of you is divorced, it is possible that you could have a civil ceremony followed by a blessing in a church. (See the chapter Second Time Around for further details.)

What Documents Should You Bring?

For all ceremonies, both partners will be asked to bring some documentation. Be warned! If you give any false information it is a criminal offence.

You will need to provide the following:

- Names and addresses, fathers' names and occupations (this can be left blank if it's not applicable).

- If either partner is under 23, a birth certificate will be necessary.

- For second marriages evidence of the end of the marriage is necessary. This can be either a death certificate or decree absolute. No uncertified documents will be accepted.

If any of the documents are in a foreign language you'll need a certified translation in English. You will have to get this from an approved translator. Translators can tell you if they have approval to do a certified translation.

At What Age Can You Marry?

If you are 16 or 17 you will need parental consent. If consent is refused you can apply to a magistrate's court, county court or High Court for permission to marry. You should get some legal advice before you approach the court. If you want to marry within the Church of England you will not need any proof of parental consent but the vicar can't marry you if he or she is made aware of dissent. Eloping to Gretna Green is still an option for those who can't get permission in England and Wales. In Scotland and Northern Ireland the legal age of marriage is 16. A District Registrar should be the first port of call. You will need to inform him or her of your intention to marry.

Who Can't You Marry?

All immediate family like brothers, sisters, fathers, mothers, grandparents, nieces, nephews are considered, by law, too closely related to marry. For stepbrothers and stepsisters the situation is a little more complicated. In some cases stepbrothers and stepsisters can marry but not if they are under 21 or if they have lived under the same roof. Some in-laws are also out of bounds.

A former father-in-law may not marry his son's wife, for example. Adopted children cannot marry their adoptive parents, but they can marry other members of their adoptive family, even their adoptive brother or sister. First cousins can marry. If you are considering this, it might be an idea to talk to your GP so that he or she can look into your families' medical histories and explain any genetic consequences for your children.

Women cannot marry their:

▌ Grandfather

▌ Father

▌ Father's brother

▌ Father's half-brother

▌ Mother's brother

▌ Mother's half-brother

▌ Adoptive father

▌ Brother

▌ Half-brother

▌ Son

▌ Adopted son

- Sister's son

- Half-sister's son

- Brother's son

- Half-brother's son

- Grandson

Men cannot marry their:

- Grandmother

- Mother

- Mother's sister

- Mother's half sister

- Father's sister

- Father's half-sister

- Adoptive mother

- Sister

- Half-sister

- Daughter

- Adopted daughter

- Sister's daughter

- Half-sister's daughter

▌ Brother's daughter

▌ Half-brother's daughter

▌ Granddaughter

Do I Have to Change My Name?

No. Women are under no legal obligation to change their names to that of their husband. If you do decide to change your name (men can too) you need to remember to change official documents. The important ones to remember are: bank account details, driving licence, passport, life assurance, notifying your employer, your pension fund, any investments, doctors, dentists, council tax, library, tax office, mortgage lender and credit card. For women who don't want to change their name to Mrs it's possible to become Ms officially. To amend a passport you will find the relevant passport form at any main post office.

Marrying Overseas

Marriages in foreign countries are recognized in the UK provided they do not contravene the laws of eligibility (such as polygamous marriages and those between immediate family members) in the UK.

If you are in any doubt about the legal standing of a marriage, ring the embassy of the country in which you are intending to marry before booking. Make sure you have a record of your marriage taking place abroad. Couples can register their marriages at British consulates overseas – papers will be passed back to the Registrar General so the couple are registered in Britain. Alternatively, on your return, the original marriage certificate or a certified copy can be registered with the Family Records Centre. If you ever lose your marriage certificate, it is easier to get a copy from here than from St Lucia or New Zealand.

If you are marrying a foreign national abroad you will sometimes be able to acquire your other half's nationality on marriage. This does not usually mean you lose British citizenship, although some countries do not allow dual nationality – so this should be checked before marriage.

Other Legal Issues

What do I do if my partner lives abroad?
If one partner lives abroad the marriage has to wait until the foreign partner has fulfilled the necessary residency arrangements. Spouses of British citizens may apply to join their husband or wife in Britain as long as the British partner is settled in the UK – settled means living here lawfully with no time limit on your stay. You will need to prove that, as a couple, you can support yourselves and any dependants without relying on state help and that you have a genuine relationship. For further information write or telephone the Immigration and Nationality Department:

Immigration and Nationality Department
Lunar House
40 Wellesley Road
Croydon
Surrey CR9 2BY

Tel: 08706 067766 (calls are answered in turn so wait for a reply).

What do I do if my partner lives in Scotland and we want to marry in England or Wales?
If you want to marry in England and Wales but your partner lives in Scotland, the Scottish resident must obtain a

certificate of no impediment or a certificate of proclamation of banns in the Church of Scotland. Then normal procedure should be followed.

What do I do if my partner lives in N. Ireland and we want to marry in England or Wales?
If you want to marry in England and Wales, the partner who lives in N. Ireland must obtain a certificate from the District Registrar of Marriages in N. Ireland or arrange for the banns.

4 *What Type of Wedding?*

Although uttering the words 'I do' will probably be one of the most romantic things you will ever say in your life, there are some feet-on-the-ground practicalities to becoming man and wife. This chapter gets down to basics and looks at the multitude of possible ways of marrying.

To narrow down the field, your first decision should be whether you want a religious or civil wedding. Then depending on how quickly you want to marry (the fastest method being one clear day's notice) you can choose the most appropriate type of service. Think about costs. Decide whether you want a formal or informal wedding and then start contacting the right people to set the marriage ceremony wheels in motion.

Religious Weddings

Church of England/Church in Wales Weddings

If you are marrying within the Church of England or Church in Wales, your first port of call will be the vicar of your or your partner's parish. He or she will want to discuss with you the spiritual and emotional implications of tying the knot and could suggest you undertake a marriage preparation course to prepare you for the biggest step of your life.

Every marriage in England and Wales must be announced or licensed before the service can legally take place. In the

Church of England the announcement is called the banns. Banns must be read out in your parish church or churches on three Sundays before the wedding, the intention being to give plenty of time for live spouses to crawl out of the woodwork and declare the marriage unfit. It is normal for the couple to attend church at least once when the banns are read out. The marriage must take place within three months of the reading out of the banns.

If you cannot wait to race up the aisle, marriage by common licence is a much quicker method. Once approved by the Bishop of your diocese or his appointee, you only have to wait one clear day before you can wed. This is not a standard marriage licence. You must have a pretty valid reason for needing to get married so quickly, like having to go overseas urgently.

If you do not want to or cannot tie the knot in your own parish church(es), a special licence is needed. You will need a good reason, not 'I've seen this gorgeous little country church ...'. Perhaps if your mother and grandmother were married in a particular church or a member of your close family lives in a particular district. This licence has to be approved by the Archbishop of Canterbury and is issued from the Court of Faculties, No. 1 The Sanctuary, Westminster, London SW1P 3JT (tel: 0171 222 5381). You also need this licence to marry in a building that is not approved for marriage. Even the royal family has to apply for a special licence to wed in St Paul's!

Finally, it is possible to be married by Superintendent Registrar's Certificate Without Licence. This method will only be granted in special cases such as a divorcee marrying outside his or her parish. The church where the couple marries must be in the same registration district as the Superintendent Registrar.

With so much choice you can't put a foot wrong.

At Rainbow we not only offer a divine collection of fashionable shoes, we also offer them in any colour you desire.

It is by providing this kind of personal, tailor-made service that has made us Europe's leading specialist.

So step into a world of colour and style.

CLUB

Marrying colour with style

01392 207030

Costs

There are two sets of prices. The first are national fixed prices for the marriage service and the banns. The second are charges decided by the parochial church council. These are for costs at the church, like lighting, heating, choir, organist, bells and flowers. It may also be necessary to pay a verger's fee if a verger is required at the ceremony. Your minister will be able to advise you what the current charges are.

Fixed prices:

▌ Banns   £14;

▌ Certificate of Banns   £8 (needed to prove that the banns have been read in your local parish);

▌ Marriage service   £127.

Charges for other costs such as the choir and organist are decided by parochial church council. Charges vary for each council.

Jewish Weddings

For a Jewish wedding you need to make two applications, religious and civil. The legal requirements are the same as those for a civil wedding other than that Jewish weddings do not have to take place between 8 am and 6 pm. To fulfil the religious aspect, you will need to make a separate application to the religious authority that has jurisdiction over your ceremony. You will be required to show documents that prove your identity and the fact that you are Jewish. For example, your parents' Jewish marriage licence.

Usually the secretary of the synagogue will be licensed to keep a marriage register. If this is not the case a Superintendent Registrar will have to attend the wedding. By law

Jewish marriages can take place anywhere, although rabbinical law states that the ceremony must take place under a _chuppah_.

Roman Catholic Weddings

Similarly, Roman Catholic weddings need two applications, religious and civil. The legal requirements are the same as those for a civil wedding. You will need a good couple of months to organize all the necessities, so approach your priest as soon as possible. If both partners are Roman Catholic, banns can be published. If one of you is of a different faith, the priest of the Roman Catholic partner will grant a dispensation to allow the marriage to take place in a Catholic church.

Further inquiries to The Catholic Inquiry office, The Chase Centre, 114 West Heath Road, London, NW3 7TX (tel: 0181 458 3316).

What About Other Religious Weddings?

The legal requirements are the same as those of a civil wedding. If the place of worship is in a different registration district than where you live, you will usually need either to prove that you regularly attend the place of worship or to give notice in the registration district where you want to be married.

Civil Marriages

You will both have to give notice at your local register office regardless of whether you are marrying within your district. Once the Superintendent Registrar has agreed the marriage you can marry in any register office in any district.

There are two methods:

▌ The first is to marry by Certificate Without Licence. Your notice of marriage will be entered in the marriage notice book and should state where you will wed. Then 21 days after the entry in the book, you can marry. The certificate without licence is valid for 12 months. This option is only possible if both partners have lived in England or Wales for the seven days before giving notice.

▌ The second method is to marry by Certificate and Licence (also known as Special Licence). Once you have given notice at your local register office, the Superintendent Registrar can issue the certificate and licence. This enables you to marry one clear day after entry in the marriage notice book as long as that day is not a Sunday, Christmas Day or Good Friday. This second option is possible if one partner has lived in England or Wales for 15 days before giving notice.

What if my partner cannot attend a licensed venue?
A Registrar's General Licence allows a marriage to take place at any time and anywhere. It can be obtained for people too ill to leave home or hospital. Unlike other civil weddings, there are no residency requirements and it is possible to obtain this licence immediately. The marriage must take place within 12 months of entry into the marriage notice book.

Costs

▌ Marriage certificate issued by registrar   £3.50;

▌ Marriage certificate deposited with Superintendent Registrar   £6.50;

- Entry in marriage notice book   £23;

- Licence for marriage   £46.50;

- Registrar attending marriage at a register office   £32;

- Registrar to attend marriage outside a register office £36.

NB: These costs apply when a couple live in the same registration district. If not, the costs of a register office marriage are £78 in total. The cost of marriage for a couple in the same registration district is £55 (giving notice plus registrar's fee £32). In different registration districts each member of the couple must pay to give notice (£23 + £23 + registrar's fee £32).

Marriage in Scotland

In Scotland, the quickest possible marriage is 15 days after giving notice. This applies for religious and civil weddings. However, the process can take longer, so notice should be handed in about four weeks before you want to marry. Leave yourself at least six weeks if it's your second marriage.

Both partners must submit a marriage notice to the registrar of the district in which they want to marry. When the registrar is happy that all the documentation is correct he or she will provide a marriage schedule, which enables the marriage to proceed. In a civil marriage the registrar will bring the marriage schedule along to the ceremony. After signature he or she will register the marriage.

There are the same requirements for a religious marriage, although it's a good idea to visit your vicar or clergyman before submitting a notice of marriage. The only difference is that either the bride or groom must pick up the marriage schedule from the registrar before the marriage.

This will only be possible seven days before the ceremony. You will then need to give the marriage schedule to the authorized person carrying out the ceremony. It must be signed immediately after the marriage by the bride and groom and by the witnesses. Within three days it should be returned to the registrar in order to legally register the marriage.

Costs

▌ For each person submitting a notice of marriage (civil and religious) to the District Registrar   £12;

▌ For solemnization of a civil marriage   £45;

▌ For each extract of the entry in the register of marriages £8.

Two people could give notice of marriage, have a civil marriage solemnized by the registrar and have one extract of the register entry (their marriage certificate) for the total statutory fees of £77. Local authorities can add additional fees depending on the facilities available.

Marriage in Northern Ireland

Church of Ireland

Marriage in the Church of Ireland can be authorized through several methods if either or both the bride and groom are members of the Church of Ireland or other Protestant or Episcopal Church.

Firstly, a licence can be issued if one member of the couple has lived for at least seven days in the licensing minister's district before giving notice of marriage.

Secondly, a Special Licence can be granted by a Bishop of the Church, for which there is a fixed fee set by the church authorities. This is issued when a couple want to marry outside both their parishes. There must be a good reason. For example, one of the couple grew up in the parish in which they want to wed, or one of the couple has close family ties to the parish.

Thirdly, if one of the couple is a member of the Church of Ireland and has lived for 14 days prior to marriage in the appropriate district, they may marry by Registrar's Certificate.

The final method, publication of banns, is only possible when both bride and groom are members of the Church of Ireland or other Protestant Episcopal Church. Banns are published in the church(es) of the parish(es) in which both parties live, three Sundays in advance of the wedding. This must be arranged with the minister(s) seven days before they are announced.

Presbyterian

For Presbyterian weddings, if one or both parties are Presbyterian it is possible to marry by licence if notice is given to the minister of a congregation where he or she has been a member for one month.

The minister may then issue a certificate that confirms the giving of notice, which will then have to be given to the licensing minister. Seven days after receipt of this certificate, the licensing minister can issue a licence that authorizes the marriage.

A Special Licence allows you to marry at any time or place in Ireland and is granted by one of the four main governing bodies: The General Assembly of the Presbyterian Church in Ireland, The Remonstrant Synod of Ulster, The Presbytery of Antrim and The Reformed Presbyterian Synod of Ireland. The fee is fixed by the church authorities.

Banns can be published when both parties are Presbyterian. Publication of banns must be made on three Sundays before the marriage. You will need to give six days' notice to the minister. Banns are published in the churches of the bride and groom and the marriage must take place in one of the churches in which the banns were read.

Roman Catholic

Roman Catholics can marry by licence if one or both of the couple are Roman Catholic. The licence can be obtained from a licensor appointed by a Bishop. If only one of the couple is Roman Catholic, allow seven days before the licence is issued.

A Registrar's Certificate is available if one of the couple is not Roman Catholic. A Registrar's Certificate gives permission for a marriage to take place in a Roman Catholic Church within the registration district of the certificate.

Jewish

Jewish weddings can take place by a Registrar's Certificate. There are no residency requirements and the wedding may take place within any district in N. Ireland.

Civil Marriages

Civil marriages and those of other denominations can take place by three methods.

Firstly, by Registrar's Licence (except for Jewish weddings and the Society of Friends); if one of the couple lives in the district a registrar can authorize a marriage in any licensed premises in that district. The registrar can issue the licence seven clear days after giving notice.

If you live in the same registration district, one of you will need to have been resident for at least 15 days, and the other for 7 days immediately prior to giving notice of marriage.

If you live in different districts, notice of marriage must be given to the registrar of both districts. In this instance both of you must have been residents in your districts for 15 days immediately prior to giving notice. The registrar of the district within which the marriage will take place must receive the certificate from the registrar of the other district before he or she can issue a licence.

Secondly, you can marry by Registrar's Certificate; if both or one of you lives within a registration district, the registrar can issue a licence in any licensed premises in that district. If both parties live in the same district they must both have lived there for at least seven days immediately before giving notice. If the couple live in different districts then they also must have lived in their districts for at least seven days prior to giving notice. Notice should be given to the registrar of each district. Twenty-one clear days after notice is given, the registrar(s) can issue the certificate(s). In both cases, the registrar must also send copies of the notice to the minister of the church where the wedding will take place and to the ministers of the bride and groom's regular places of worship.

Costs

Church of Ireland or Presbyterian Church
Notice of marriage   £8.50
Licence   £10.50

Civil Marriages
Notice of marriage   £8.50
Licence   £10.50
Certificate   £5.50
Marriage solemnized in the presence of the registrar   £12.50

Marriage on the Authority of a Licence Issued by the Registrar General
Notice of marriage   £8.50
Attendance of Registrar of Marriages at a person's residence to take notice of marriage   £18

Licence   £10.50
Attendance of Registrar of Marriages at a person's residence
for the purpose of Solemnization of Marriage   £18
Solemnization of Marriage by Registrar of Marriages   £8.50

NB: Some of these fees will be waived if you are in receipt
of income support benefit.

5 Planning for the Costs

The reason why this chapter comes before the chapters on where you plan to marry and the type of wedding you want is that costs will pay a major role in your plans.

The average cost of a wedding is now £11,111, according to *Wedding and Home* magazine. However, some weddings can easily cost double that amount – particularly if there are a large number of guests to wine and dine.

Few brides want to compromise on their 'dream' of what their wedding day will be like, yet many are forced to because financial resources are stretched. Increasingly the financial burden does not fall on just the father of the bride. More and more couples either contribute towards or pay the full costs of their own nuptials.

So how can you ensure that you not only have enough cash to pay for your big day, but also avoid any arguments about who will pay for what?

How Much Will It Cost?

It is possible to get married for as little as £78 plus the cost of getting to the register office and back! So your wedding does not have to cost a fortune.

While many parents and couples save up for the big day, this may not always be possible. It is important to do your sums before planning your wedding so that the costs can be tailored to what you can afford. The easiest way to do this is to add up:

▌ any savings or money you have set aside to pay for the wedding;

▌ the amount either the parents of the bride or both parents have said they are willing to contribute;

▌ how much additional cash you expect to have saved up before the wedding day.

Then work out a rough budget for the wedding to see if there is a shortfall. It should look something like this:

My Wedding Budget

Wedding stationery	£_____
Wedding ceremony (allow roughly £3,000 for a full-blown church wedding and roughly £78 upwards for a register office ceremony. Don't forget to include flowers, music, etc)	£_____
Reception costs (tailor this to what you can afford – a reception at home can cost as little as £7.50 a head but generally you should budget for around £25–30 per person including drinks)	£_____
Bride's dress	£_____
Groom's outfit	£_____
Cars	£_____
Flowers	£_____
Rings	£_____
Photographer/video	£_____
Cake	£_____
Going-away outfit	£_____
Honeymoon	£_____
TOTAL	£_____

Now that you have a rough idea of how much cash you have available to spend and a provisional budget, you will know if there is a shortfall and how big this is. Unless your parents have money set aside or you have had a windfall, this is probably the case.

See the section on 'Savings' later in this chapter for tips on the best ways to raise the cash.

Who Will Pay For What?

To avoid arguments it is best to sit down with your families to decide who will foot the bill for what.

Now that you have a good idea of what you expect your wedding to cost, you may find that the bride's parents or both parents can afford to pay for the whole day. However, this is less and less common today. In fact more than half of all couples pay for the entire cost of their wedding party.

If you are agreeing to share the financial burden of the big day, make sure that each family member keeps his or her promise. Rather than insisting on seeing a cheque, a more sensible approach may be to set up a wedding savings account so that each person can make a contribution.

If you and your family need to save up, make sure that money is paid over before the wedding day. The last thing you will want upon arriving at the church is a row over who will pay for the car.

Remember, most couples hugely under-estimate the costs of their wedding, so make sure you have some contingency funds or access to some short-term borrowing such as an overdraft just in case there is a shortfall.

The Traditional Approach

Traditionally, the bride's parents pay for the engagement announcement, the bride's dress, the attendants' clothing, flowers for the wedding reception and venue, the photographs, the wedding video, invitations (place-setting cards and order-of-service cards), the transport and the reception. The groom pays for the costs of church or register office, honeymoon, engagement and wedding rings, presents for the best man and the attendants, transport to honeymoon, bouquets and corsages.

However, as more couples marry later in life when they are already financially independent, many parents either expect – or hope because of financial constraints – that their children will at least pay part of the bill.

Be Realistic

It is quite natural for a bride to want her 'dream' wedding and for her parents to fulfil their traditional obligations of paying for a lavish reception. However, it is also essential that you are realistic. Do you really want your parents to struggle financially just so that you can have an expensive champagne instead of sparkling wine? And do you want to put your relationship under additional strain because you are starting married life in debt?

Remember that cutting costs does not necessarily mean cutting corners.

Cost-cutting Tips

Reception

This is usually the biggest expense. If cash is tight consider the following:

- A buffet instead of the traditional 'wedding breakfast'.

- A venue that allows you to provide your own catering or your own wine.

■ Being creative in terms of the venue – for example, transforming a local church hall with drapes of fabric and hired tables and chairs or renting a non-traditional wedding venue such as a school hall.

■ Holding the reception at your parent's home – particularly if there is room in the garden for a marquee.

Dresses and suits

■ Hire instead of buy.

■ Get a friend or relative to make them instead of buying them off the shelf.

Transport

■ Restrict the number of hire cars to just one.

Photography

■ A popular trend is to buy cheap disposable cameras and give them to several of the guests to take informal photographs.

■ Hire or borrow a camcorder to video the big day rather than paying a professional.

■ Restrict the number of professional photographs – you usually pay for the number of prints that you want.

Stationery

■ Write, type or make your own invitations, place cards and hymn sheets.

Remember, a low-budget wedding does not have to mean warm white wine and dried-up sandwiches in a room above your local pub.

Financing Your Wedding

First, decide how much money you need to raise to pay for the entire wedding day and honeymoon. Then agree who will pay for what and how much will be paid by the parents and how much by the couple.

Also, decide on an overall budget for the wedding. Couples generally hugely under-estimate the cost of weddings, so keep a close eye on your costs.

Now you know how much cash you need to raise.

Most couples will have saved around £7,250 before their big day according to *Wedding and Home* magazine. However, if you both put £50 aside each month it will take some six years to build up a lump sum that large! So, unless you happen to have a cash injection from your parents or have already built up some joint savings, you will probably have to look at a mixture of the following ways to finance your wedding.

Savings

The longer you have before the big day, the easier it will be to save and the more chance that your money will grow.

Fewer than 30 per cent of couples use a savings account that pays interest. Even though interest rates are relatively low, it is still worth getting any extra income you can. Shop around for the best rates.

Also, be aware that if you set up a joint account you can both withdraw cash from this account. This can lead to arguments if one of you decides to spend some of the savings without the other's agreement. So before opening the account set some parameters – who can withdraw cash/ write cheques, what is the maximum one of you will spend without telling the other, how much will you both pay in and who will make sure you are on target to build up the required level of savings.

Another alternative is to set up an ISA – or Individual Savings Account. You can both set one up and invest up to £3,000 in savings each year and receive interest free of tax. You can get hold of your money fairly quickly and as there is tough competition among ISA providers you can usually earn a far higher rate of interest than in a conventional savings account.

Borrowing

If you do not have enough money saved for the big day, you can always borrow some of the costs.

The best ways to borrow will depend not only on how much cash you need to raise, but also how quickly you hope to repay this debt.

Credit cards

Your credit card is only suitable for shorter-term borrowing of around six months or less. If you want to pay for one aspect of the wedding – for example, the honeymoon, dress, reception – on a credit card make sure that you shop around for a card with a low rate of interest.

Remember, if you have a joint credit card, you are both jointly liable for any debts. So if one of you goes on a spending spree without the other's agreement it could not only lead to rows but one of you could end up paying for the other's indulgences.

Overdraft

Again, this is only suitable for short-term borrowing. Remember, an overdraft can be withdrawn by your bank at any time. The rates charged can also be high – particularly if you exceed your agreed overdraft limit.

Loans

Taking out a loan will be a good idea if you plan to repay the debt over 12 months or more. Shop around for a competitive rate. There will be a trade-off between monthly repayments and the length of the loan. The longer the loan the lower the amount you repay each month, but generally the higher the total interest bill.

Mortgage

As many couples already cohabit, which means that they often already have a mortgage, they should also consider increasing the size of their home loan. Not only are mortgages one of the cheapest ways to borrow, but as the loan is being paid off over so many years (usually 25) the monthly costs are also low.

Financial Tips

Keep track of everything that needs to be paid for, what you are expecting to pay, what you actually pay and whether you are over or under budget.

Good organization is vital. With so many bits of paperwork to keep track of, you do not want to lose the reception venue to another couple because you forgot to pay the deposit.

Remember that the first few months of marriage can be quite stressful. Once the honeymoon period is over, you do not want to be arguing over money. So instead of trying to pay for your wedding quickly, consider taking out a loan or increasing the size of your mortgage – that way you will have lower monthly repayments.

Also, see the chapters: Wedding Insurance and Organizing Your Married Finances.

6 *Picking the Date*

Having decided to take the plunge, the next step is to pick a date. While a massive extravaganza with a church wedding and 200 guests is a campaign requiring months of intricate planning, a simple register office affair with a few friends and some drinks at the pub afterwards can be organized in days.

Timing

For a formal wedding there are loads of time-consuming considerations. You and your wedding party will have to arrange transport, catering, a venue, music, clothes, hair and flowers, and that's just the start of it.

It's not only planning for you – guests have to find an outfit, get their hair done and make travel arrangements.

Also, bear in mind how many other couples are planning to wed on the same day. Churches, reception venues, photographers and caterers tend to be very busy during the summer – the most popular time to marry. Some 100,000 couples tie the knot in just the few months between July and September.

Quick Weddings

For shotgun weddings, the fastest method available in the UK is by licence at a register office and will take two days. So you can propose on Monday and wed on Wednesday.

For a church wedding the first available date will depend on the church's popularity and forthcoming engagements. The banns (the official announcement of your intention to wed) will have to be read out for three Sundays before you marry.

If you want to marry outside your parish in an idyllic church in the country, that will take even longer as you'll have to apply to the Archbishop of Canterbury for a special dispensation.

How to Choose Your Big Day

Busy Days

Nowadays the majority of weddings take place on Saturdays from April to September. So, your guests may have other weddings to attend on these days. Florists, photographers, venues and caterers will be inundated at this time.

Dream venues are snapped up quickly, so make sure yours is free on your chosen date. Some are even booked up two years in advance.

You might have to put yourselves on a waiting list for all sorts of wedding essentials. So, if perfection is important, give yourself plenty of time.

Most people prefer to marry on Saturday. A weekday date or even a Sunday will provide you with a greater choice of venues. The downside of a weekday is that some of your guests will be unable to attend.

Think About Your Guests

Liaise with your family and friends. Find out if there are any dates that are inconvenient for them. Try to include your in-laws as much as possible in the decision making and choose a date that suits everyone. Think about birthdays and especially children's birthdays and school holidays (they could make it more difficult for people with children to attend).

Although a summer wedding is glorious, do not choose a day when friends and family are likely to be on holiday. Similarly, if it is too near Christmas or Easter your guests might have difficulty in attending.

Narrow Down the Odds

British weather can play havoc with your impeccably arranged wedding. Check which months have the worst rainfall levels and even winds – a gale force wind makes wearing a veil no picnic.

Think about national and international sporting events and avoid embarrassments like the groom's party sneaking off to see the World Cup Final in the middle of the reception.

Also, consider dates that are relevant to the area in which you are marrying. Don't book a church in Wimbledon on the day of the men's final, or a register office in Ascot during the season.

Your Special Day

Each day of the year has a particular significance. You might want to wed on a relevant saint's day or Valentine's day. Remember this day will be your wedding anniversary for the rest of your lives. So, ensure it's one you want to remember.

Stress Busters

▌ If you want to wed in a particular church or have the reception at a favourite venue, ask how far ahead you'll need to book.

▌ Check with friends and relatives, find out which days they can't make.

▌ Check forthcoming dates for national and international sporting events.

▌ Don't wed on or around a major religious festival.

▌ Check local events.

▌ Check the average weather.

▌ Think of the significance of each day.

▌ Make sure you allocate enough time for all the arrangements.

7 *Where to Wed*

Now you understand the legal procedures for marriage and have decided on the type of ceremony you require, the next step is to decide where to marry. Your wedding day should fulfil your dreams, so leave yourself as much time as possible to pick the ideal wedding venue.

Choosing Your Venue

To find your perfect wedding venue, view as many as possible before deciding on any one place. Ask friends for recommendations of venues they have been to or heard about. Visit any venue that you are considering so that you can assess it properly.

When you finally find your dream venue, there are some things to consider before making a booking. Firstly, despite what they say, size matters. It is vital that the venue can seat all your guests comfortably.

Secondly, consider the time of day at which you are marrying and the amount of natural light in the venue. This is particularly relevant for a summer wedding. Go and see the venue at roughly the same time of day as you will be marrying, to gain an impression of the natural light in the venue.

Think about access and parking, especially for the wedding party's transport.

Photographs are usually taken outside so make sure there is room for your wedding party and guests to congregate for the photo call.

Find out if there is a reception venue nearby, or indeed if your venue is a wedding and reception venue in one. The latter will cut down on transport costs and makes it easy for the guests and the wedding party if they can walk to the reception from the wedding.

Also, think about the first night. Find out if there is a suitable place to stay nearby or if you could stay at the wedding venue itself. This can be cost efficient as some venues offer package deals.

Booking Your Venue

Try to book as far in advance as possible, as popular venues are booked up quickly. Always discuss how long you are booking for – you don't want to be hurried at your own wedding. Finally, if you are paying for your wedding venue, ensure you have the booking in writing well in advance, with an agreed price, date and time of booking.

Religious Weddings

If you are marrying within the Church of England, Church in Wales or Roman Catholic Church, you will need a good reason to marry outside the parish(es) in which both partners live. If you both live in areas where neither of you wants to marry, consider if either of you have a family link to a church which you feel more inspired by and linked to.

For example, you might have been brought up in a parish in which you would prefer to marry or your family may have a strong connection with a different part of the UK to that in which you are living. In which case you could apply for a special licence to allow you to marry outside your parish (see chapter on the legal requirements of marriage).

For Jewish weddings there is a lot more freedom. As long as the rabbi approves the venue, marriage can take place anywhere under a *chuppah*. This could be at home, in the garden or just about anywhere – see our tips on civil weddings.

Civil Weddings

Newly Licensed Premises

For those who are having a civil wedding, the possibilities of where to marry are now much greater than your local register office. Nowadays you can marry in any licensed venue across the UK, from a zoo to a roller coaster.

In March 1998 there were more than 2,000 newly licensed premises. So, if you have always dreamed of getting wed in a Merchant Ivory-style stately home or longed to say 'I do' in a wild and windy Scottish castle – all is now possible. For those who want a more alternative wedding, like a James Bond theme marriage, there are also some weird and wonderful venues now licensed.

A list of 'approved premises' is available from the Office for National Statistics. (Just send a postal order for £5 made payable to ONS to ONS, PO Box 56, Southport, PR8 2GL.)

The legal requirements are exactly the same as for a Register office. First contact the registrar for the district in which you intend to marry to arrange his or her presence at your wedding. Then notice of the marriage must be given to your local registrar.

The paperwork will be sent on to the registrar who is performing the ceremony. If you have your heart set on a particular building or beauty spot where you would like to get hitched and want to know if it's allowed, get in touch with the Superintendent Registrar in the Register office covering that area.

Tying the Knot Abroad

Many couples now avoid the British weather and get wed abroad. As foreign travel is becoming easier and easier there is a growing industry of foreign 'package weddings', with companies like Virgin Bride in association with Thomas Cook offering some great hassle-free deals.

Most specialist tour companies arrange a wedding and honeymoon in one, so there is very little for the couple to worry about, except enjoying themselves. Decide on anywhere from Mustique to Lapland but do choose a company that you are either recommended or have prior experience of. Failing that, choose a company that is ABTA (Association of British Travel Agents) bonded.

Anyone marrying abroad should make sure that they make arrangements for a copy of the marriage certificate to be logged in this country. If you do not organize this at the time it can lead to great difficulties. Most wedding insurers won't cover newly weds for loss of marriage documentation when marrying abroad. (See our chapter on the legal requirements of marriage.)

Finally, don't forget your relatives. If you do decide on marrying overseas, have a celebration of some sort when you get home so that family and friends don't feel excluded. However, do think about your family and friends carefully before you choose an overseas wedding. On one hand, package weddings are great because you avoid months of painstaking preparation. On the other hand, you might come to your wedding day and realize that you would love your nearest and dearest to be there with you.

The Italian Connection

Getting married in Italy is a perfect way to tie the knot and Weddings Made in Italy was set up for the sole purpose of promoting Italy as the number one destination to get married, and also to inform people that this was now possible, and logically if booked through Weddings Made in Italy, easy and straightforward.

Why choose Italy, I hear you ask? Italy is the land of romance, love and great beauty, an idyllic location for matters of the heart and soul... need I go on? Getting married in Italy is hassle-free, we make all the arrangements for you; Cost-effective - wedding packages are catered to your budget; A neutral meeting point - if family and friends have to travel to be there anyway, why not select Italy which provides an enjoyable getaway for everyone; A time-saver - Most couples plan their wedding 12 months in advance and for a wedding in Italy all the time you need to decide is 6 months; Second weddings - a perfect way to have a simple wedding. Getting married in Italy also provides couples with the opportunity to break away from the traditional British wedding, reduce costs, be different and exclusive and break away from the mass wedding ceremonies which are now available throughout the Caribbean and the Pacific.

What is so different about Weddings Made in Italy? The main difference is that we are first and foremost your wedding consultants and wedding co-ordinators. We listen to your needs and requirements and then provide you with the options we feel are relevant to your needs. We can tailor-make your wedding to suit your budget. Our main travel company - The Italian Connection (London) can also assist you with all your travel arrangements to Italy - be it an elegant villa or a simple pensione tucked away in the Tuscan countryside.

There are 3 ways to get married in Italy:

1. **The Civil Wedding** - This can only take place in a town hall. The town halls in Italy are quite beautiful and range from the Palazzo Vecchio in Florance to the Campidolio or the Terme di Caracalla in Rome, you can also be married in the garden of the Town Hall in Sorrento or the terrace in Positano. It is possible to arrange civil ceremonies throughout Italy and dates can only be confirmed 6 months beforehand.

2. **The Catholic wedding** - We have a range of beautiful churches throughout Italy, small and quaint, large and dramatic, baroque and renaissance, elegant and charming... the list is endless. There are a range of difficulties regarding catholic weddings and this is based on the paperwork which needs to take place here in the UK and in Italy. There are certain places in Italy where a Catholic Wedding is not possible and this is due to a series of papal directives.

3. The Anglican/Protestant wedding - In my opinion this is the best possibility available for couples wanting to get married in Italy. It allows couples total flexibility. Couples can get married in a villa, castle, terrace, garden, hotel, the possibilities are endless. We have designed packages to assist you with this and they range from weddings in Villa Cora - a baroque display of colour and splendour, a Venetian Palace close to St. Marks, the Basilica di Santi Cosma e Damiani in Rome in the heart of the Eternal city, the splendid gardens of the Murat in the centre of Positano overlooking the dome of the Cattedrale. Weddings Made in Italy has total exclusivity and this wedding is recognised both on a civil and religious basis.

Apart from the preparations, the paperwork, witness, interpreter and ceremony Weddings Made in Italy offers a range of subsidiary services.

Flowers (bouquets and boutonnieres), a limousine wedding service and where possible we can also arrange a horse and cart for you, or if you decide to get married in Venice why not follow in the steps of Woody Allen and go for a transfer by speedboat or stick to tradition and arrive at the ceremony by gondola. We also have photographers on site or available from here, musicians ranging from opera singer to a violinist or choral choir, a hairdresser and make-up artist is available in every location. Then comes the wedding reception which can be as simple and rustic or as elegant and flamboyant as you require. We can cater for a minimum of 2 people to a maximum of 500. We can arrange everything for you from the flower arrangements and decorations to the bomboniere, the fireworks display to the music, the menus to the wedding cake......

There is also a pre-preparatory stage which can help you select the right wedding dress or attire. Why not fly out to Florence and choose the dress or outfit of your dreams, we can pick you up from the airport and whisk you off to a selection of different shops where you will be able to select you shoes, tiara, rings and various accessories. Alternatively our dressmakers can also fly out to visit you.

Weddings Made in Italy is now launching and taking bookings for its Millennium Weddings. It is now possible to book for this special event. Celebrate the Millennium with a Millennium wedding with a difference or why not contact The Italian Connection (London) and let us tailor-make the perfect honeymoon to Italy for you. Whether you are looking for romantic spa cottages, complete escapism, scuba diving, 3-10 day cruises, islands, lakes or mountains... The Italian Connection (London) will be able to head you in the right direction.

Italy is the perfect place for a new beginning.

Stress Busters

▌ View all possible venues for your wedding.

▌ Consider the amount of natural light in a venue.

▌ Think about access and parking.

▌ Clarify how long you are booking for.

▌ Find out if there is a reception venue nearby or at the wedding venue.

▌ Find out if there is a suitable first night venue nearby or at the wedding venue.

8 *Organizing Your Time*

To get hitched without a hitch there are only three things you have to remember: planning, planning and planning. A traditional wedding will need at least six months' planning time, and with so much to do, a timetable and check-list are vital.

Firstly, write down all the jobs to be done. Think about the decisions you will have to make by a certain date and who has been allocated what job and its deadline.

Countdown to Your Big Day

After the Engagement

▍ Tell friends and family of your intention to marry.

▍ Announce your engagement in local and/or national newspapers.

▍ Decide on a civil or a religious wedding.

▍ Visit your priest or rabbi to discuss the wedding.

▍ Decide on a formal or informal wedding.

▍ Sit down with both sets of in-laws, make a rough draft of your joint wedding guests and decide on the size of the wedding and the reception.

▌ Also, with your in-laws organize a total budget – set a top amount that you are not going to exceed.

▌ Gather estimates and choose a location for the wedding and reception (register offices can only give a provisional booking; the final booking needs to be made three months before the wedding).

▌ Find a suitable date when the wedding and reception venues are free and book them (make sure you book far enough ahead to give yourself time for all the arrangements).

▌ Choose the wedding party, best man, chief bridesmaid, etc.

▌ Meet with your wedding party and allocate jobs.

▌ Start looking for a dress; if it's something very special book now.

▌ If so inclined, brides could start thinking about diets or changing hairstyles now.

Six to Three Months Prior to Wedding

▌ Choose your wedding dress.

▌ Choose accessories like shoes and jewellery.

▌ Choose outfits for the bride's attendants.

▌ Choose outfits for the groom, ushers and best man if buying.

▌ Start looking for a wedding ring.

▮ Give notice of your wedding to the register office and confirm the date of wedding three months prior to the event. Check what facilities the wedding venue has for music and organize your wedding music.

▮ Visit your minister or rabbi again to confirm the date of publication of the banns and confirm the type of service you are having, which prayer book, etc. Also choose the music and meet and book the organist, choir and bell-ringers (if applicable). Have the music approved by the minister.

▮ Order your wedding cake, or start making it now if it's a fruit cake.

▮ Order invitations and the order-in-service sheets (if applicable); check proofs.

▮ Book a photographer and/or video maker.

▮ Book the flowers, choose and organize the type of arrangements you want for the wedding venue, the headdress, and any for the wedding party; order any rare flowers now.

▮ Book transport.

▮ Book caterers for the reception. Plan the menu and include alternatives for special dietary requirements like vegetarians.

▮ Book the music for the reception.

▮ Book the honeymoon.

▮ Start to think about the bride's going away outfit.

■ Book the hotel for the wedding night.

■ Book wedding insurance.

■ Send out invitations 8–12 weeks before the wedding.

Two Months Before

■ Buy the wedding ring(s).

■ Groom's party should book morning suits if they are hiring them.

■ Organize a date for the wedding rehearsal if you're having one.

■ Have vaccinations for the honeymoon.

■ Make sure your passports are OK. The bride's should be sent off now if she's changing her name.

■ Visit a beautician and decide on hair and make-up looks for the wedding.

■ Confirm all your bookings now and tidy up any loose ends.

■ Order drink and hired glasses.

■ Finish off any fittings for bride's and attendants' clothes.

■ Polish up all clothes accessories now.

■ Buy some presents for the best man and his attendants.

■ Ask chief bridesmaid and best man to organize hen and stag nights.

One Month Before

▌ Buy the certificate or licence from the registrar. (Usually groom's responsibility.)

▌ Arrange luggage for honeymoon.

▌ Book appointments for hair and nails the day before the wedding.

▌ Check that all of the wedding party know their responsibilities.

▌ Write to any guests who haven't replied and find out if they received their invitations.

▌ Send out invites to members of the reserve list.

▌ Have the hen night and stag night.

▌ Check all the speeches have been prepared.

Two to One Week Before

▌ Organize last-minute alterations of the bride's and groom's and attendants' clothes. Weight often yo-yos around a wedding so give time to make all necessary changes.

▌ Write to the caterer confirming the exact number of guests, including details of vegetarians etc.

▌ Organize your seating plan.

▌ Bridegroom: sort out payment of officials like the minister, verger, bell-ringers, organist and choir in cash.

If not paying them himself, he should place the money in marked brown paper envelopes for the best man to distribute on the day.

▎ Make sure the going away outfit is complete and ready.

▎ Arrange for or decorate the cake and make sure it can be delivered to reception venue on the wedding day.

▎ Have a wedding rehearsal.

▎ Confirm the tickets for the honeymoon.

▎ Wrap the gifts for the best man and attendants.

▎ Collect any remaining wedding stationery.

▎ Make sure drinks are delivered.

▎ Organize collection of hired drinks, crockery, cutlery and glasses.

▎ Confirm with your photographer that he or she knows exactly what type of shots you want.

The Day Before

▎ Press or iron all the wedding clothes and lay them out the night before.

▎ Give presents to the best man and his attendants.

▎ Have hair and nails done.

▌ Pack honeymoon luggage.

▌ Go to bed early and try to relax.

The Big Day

▌ Get up as late as possible and eat a good breakfast.

▌ Supervise or help decorate the reception venue.

▌ Make sure the cake has been delivered to the venue.

▌ Make sure the flowers in the church and/or the venue are ready.

A fantastic computer software package called 'Wedding Planner' is now available. It provides tables that include everything from a budget planner to invitation templates and the reception table plan. Wedding Planner is available from Global Software Publishing on (44) 01480 496 575.

Get Some Help

If you have some extra cash and you don't want the bother, why not pay someone else to organize the whole affair for you? There are many experienced companies that provide a one-to-one service with an experienced wedding organizer who will take over as much or as little as you like. For example, Alternative Occasions – 172 Brox Road, Ottershaw, Surrey KT16 OLQ (tel: 01932 872115) – provide wedding information and advice, wedding co-ordination, party planning and venue finding. They specialize in theme weddings and have contacts with couture wedding dress designers, florists and photographers.

Stress Busters

▌ Start planning at least six months in advance.

▌ Write a six-month planner including jobs to be done and days to finalize them.

▌ Book florist, wedding and reception venues, etc as much in advance as possible.

▌ Give each job a definite deadline.

9 A Helping Hand – Who Does What

The main players in your wedding – including the best man and the bridesmaids – are not just there for traditional reasons. They will have a major role helping to organize your wedding, at the ceremony itself and at the reception afterwards.

Planning your wedding can be a trying time, so most importantly choose people you get on with and who you can rely on.

It is customary to have an equal number of men and women in your party. There are traditional roles for each member, so think about the relevant qualities potential key players have when choosing.

Listed below are the usual roles performed by each member of the wedding party. The roles are fairly flexible and will differ depending on the size of your wedding.

The Roles

The Bride

The bride's key role is to decide on the type of wedding and reception. Traditionally, she makes all the major decisions, although nowadays the bride and groom often do this together.

Traditionally also, the bride chooses the type of wedding ceremony. She chooses the date and time of the ceremony and decides on any hymns and/or music.

She chooses the bridesmaids and attendants. She organizes the wedding party and ensures that each member is aware of his or her role. She agrees the date and time of the wedding rehearsal.

She chooses the wedding dress, the florist and the clothes for the bridesmaids and bride's attendants. She arranges her own hair and beauty preparations and buys the bride's going away outfit. She orders the wedding cake, flowers and the photographer.

She contacts guests who haven't responded to their invitations and helps to finalize the guest list.

She chooses the reception venue, and catering type and menu. She decides on the colour scheme for the venue. She chooses the wines at the reception and the song for the first dance (often something of particular significance to the newly weds). She puts the finishing touches to the seating plan at the reception and tells the caterer the exact final number of guests.

She chooses the wedding stationery and the order-in-service sheet.

She makes the wedding list available. She writes the thank-you notes for the wedding gifts. She notifies the post office of any change of address.

The Bride's Mother

As hostess of the wedding, the bride's mother's responsibilities start with issuing the invitations to the wedding. This she does in joint name with her husband. All replies are addressed to her.

Usually she is responsible for the overall organization of the reception, although the bride may want to take part in this. She is in charge of the nitty gritty of the smooth running of this part of the wedding. She sorts out everything from the decoration of the reception venue to details like the delivery of the wedding cake and table decorations like napkins and candles.

She keeps an eye on the number of guests coming to the reception and makes sure there is no over- or under-booking. She may help sort out accommodation for guests. She also arranges for transport for the bridal party.

The Bride's Father

The bride's father goes to the church with his daughter and 'gives her away'. If the bride's father has passed away or cannot attend the wedding, it is quite normal for someone else to give the bride away. This is traditionally a male relative or friend, although there is no reason to stop the bride choosing a female friend or family member to fulfil this function.

The bride's father makes the first speech at the reception.

The Groom

In general the groom is responsible for arranging the legal and business aspects of getting wed.

He sorts out the Certificate and Licence and any related payments.

He is in charge of paying officials such as the verger, choirmaster, choir, organist and bell-ringers. These accounts should either be settled before the wedding, or the groom can place money in brown paper envelopes for the best man to distribute on the wedding day.

The groom chooses his best man and ushers. He chooses his suit for the ceremony and a going away outfit if needed.

He makes the second speech at the reception. He also organizes transport for the bride and groom after the ceremony. He books the honeymoon, ensures that both passports are in correct order and sorts out any necessary vaccinations.

Best Man

The best man keeps in close contact with the bride's family to help with organization. He aids the groom with practical arrangements.

He attends the wedding rehearsal. He accompanies the groom to the ceremony, organizes the transport and gets him to the church on time, finalizes parking arrangements and helps the groom with transport for the newly weds after the reception.

He collects the buttonholes for the groom and himself. He looks after the wedding rings until the exchange during the ceremony.

He might have to pay officials like the verger, bell-ringers, musicians, clergyman, registrar etc on the wedding day, if this has not already been done by the groom.

He sorts out the stag night. He looks after the groom's going away luggage.

At the ceremony he makes the third speech and reads out any messages from absent guests.

Chief Bridesmaid (if married she is called a Matron of Honour)

She sorts out the hen night.

She is in charge of helping the bride with wedding preparations, particularly with the bride's and attendants' clothes and accessories. On the wedding day she helps the bride to dress.

She arrives at the wedding venue with the bride's attendants and bride's mother. During the ceremony she looks after the bouquet and gives aid to a cumbersome train or veil.

She walks with the best man to the vestry to sign the wedding register.

She is also responsible for helping the bride change after the reception and looking after any going away luggage.

At the reception she can also help the best man to seat guests.

Although not traditional, it is becoming more common for the chief bridesmaid to make a speech about the bride during the reception.

Ushers

Ushers direct guests to their seats before the ceremony. They usually stand at the entrance and give out the order-in-service sheets. Particularly, they aid any elderly or disabled guests who have difficulty becoming seated.

Ushers are normally chosen from the family and friends of the couple.

10 The Guest List and Invitations

Although you do not need to finalize your guest list until the last few days before the wedding, it is important to decide on who you want to – ought to and have to – invite as soon as possible. You will need to know a rough idea of the numbers of guests when planning the ceremony and the reception.

The Guest List

Compiling your guest list should be one of the first things you do. Once you have a rough idea of numbers you can start working out budgets and the size of your wedding celebrations.

Although it may not always be possible or sensible, the traditional division of invitations is one-third for the bride and groom and one-third for each set of in-laws. It's important to invite who you want, but ultimately whoever's footing the bill should have a final say on numbers.

Make sure you have thought about a venue that can accommodate your guests *before* you send out any invites. And double double-check. People you forget will never forgive you.

Send invitations out 8–12 weeks before the wedding. Have a reserve list ready, as there are likely to be some refusals. Most people reply within about two weeks, so you should have time to send out a second batch of invites to your 'reserve list' guests.

Who to Invite

Inevitably, budget will constrain your choice. Unless you are having a tiny 'do', immediate families of the bride and groom are pretty obligatory. This includes close family like brothers, first cousins, aunts and uncles.

Invitations should be sent to everybody, including the wedding party and those whom you have invited in person. It is customary to send invites even to those who you know can't make it.

Children

Children at a wedding can be little angels or screaming devils. Some couples choose to leave them off the guest list entirely, while others welcome a family feel at the ceremony and the reception.

The ceremony itself can be boring for kids. To avoid little Johnny talking, or worse, crying throughout your vows, you could run a crèche during the ceremony or seat parents with kids at the back so they can make a quick getaway if necessary.

Alternatively, invite families only to the reception.

Partners

A general rule is that long-term relationships, particularly cohabitants, should be treated as a married couple and invited as a couple regardless of how well you know the partner.

However, deciding whether you can invite friends' partners will depend on your budget. Sometimes it just won't be possible to invite all long-standing partners because of your number constraint.

Invitations

Printing the Invitations

Unless it is a very informal wedding, wedding invitations are usually printed. Many styles are available from stationers, printers or department stores.

The wedding invitation should complement the type of wedding you have chosen. A formal wedding requires something traditional. Invitations should be printed or engraved on one side in black lettering on top-notch cream or white paper.

When choosing your invitations, ask to see samples of different typefaces. Engraving is the poshest and most expensive as it gives the best 'raised' print effect. Other options include thermographic printing and flat printing.

Wording of the Invitations

Suggested wording for formal cards:

Mr and Mrs John Smith
request the pleasure
of your company/
request the honour of
your presence at the marriage
of their daughter
Catherine
to Mr Charlie James
at St Matthew's Church, Fordingbridge
on Saturday, 6 February 1999
at 2 o'clock
and afterwards at
The Regal Hotel, Fordingbridge
RSVP
(hosts' address)

There are exceptions to the above:

Reception only:

> *Mr and Mrs John Smith*
> *request the pleasure*
> *of your company/*
> *request the honour of*
> *your presence at a reception*
> *following the marriage of their daughter*
> *Catherine*
> *to Mr Charlie James*
> *at the Regal Hotel, Fordingbridge*
> *at 6 o'clock*

If the bride's mother is widowed:

> *Mrs John Smith*
> *requests the pleasure*
> *of your company/*
> *requests the honour of*
> *your presence at the marriage*
> *of her daughter . . . .*

If the bride's father and stepmother are hosts:

> *Mr and Mrs John Smith*
> *request the pleasure*
> *of your company/*
> *request the honour of*
> *your presence at the marriage*
> *of his daughter . . . .*

If the bride's mother and stepfather are hosts:

> *Mr and Mrs Jim Richmond*
> *request the pleasure*
> *of your company/*
> *request the honour of*
> *your presence at the marriage*
> *of her daughter*

If the single host is a step-parent:

> *Mr John Smith (Mrs John Smith)*
> *requests the pleasure*
> *of your company/*
> *requests the honour of*
> *your presence at the marriage*
> *of his (her) stepdaughter Jane (can include surname if different)*

If parents are divorced but hosting the wedding:

> *Mr John Smith and Mrs Jane Smith (or if desired maiden name)*
> *request the pleasure*
> *of your company/*
> *request the honour of*
> *your presence at the marriage*
> *of their daughter*

If the single host is the bride's mother who is divorced:

> *Mrs Jane Smith*
> *requests the pleasure*
> *of your company/*
> *requests the honour of*
> *your presence at the marriage*
> *of her daughter*

If the bride's mother has remarried but is jointly hosting with the bride's father, her ex-husband:

Mr John Smith and Mrs Stephen Hill
request the pleasure
of your company/
request the honour of
your presence at the marriage
of their daughter

If the hosts are a different relation to the bride:

Mr and Mrs John Smith
request the pleasure
of your company/
request the honour of
your presence at the marriage
of their niece

If there is no family connection:

Mr Jim Jones
requests the pleasure
of your company/
request the honour of
your presence at the marriage
of Sophie Miles

If the bride and groom are the hosts:

Miss Sophie Miles and Mr Charlie Harris
request the pleasure
of your company/
request the honour of
your presence at their marriage

RSVP Address

The RSVP address is traditionally on the bottom left-hand corner of the invitation and will be that of the host or maybe the bride.

Checks Before Printing

Clarify that envelopes are included in the price. Make sure you are getting the best deal by shopping around and ask for a quote for all possible typefaces. Ask to see a proof of the invitation *before* it is printed. You will need to check that the paper colour, wording, date, spelling, punctuation, line spacing and typefacing are correct.

Addressing the Invitations

Names should be written on the top left-hand corner with an ink pen. Envelopes should be written by hand. If writing to a married couple, only the wife's name is written on the envelope. So Mr and Mrs Jim Smith on the invitation will be Mrs Jim Smith on the envelope.

Information

Think about ways of making your guests' lives easier. Maps are helpful for those unfamiliar with the territory. Details of trains and local taxis can make life easier for your guests. Including a list of possible accommodation with telephone numbers and prices is a thoughtful and useful gesture. Reply cards encourage guests to respond quicker and are becoming more common in Britain.

Seal It With a Kiss

Bridal seals and ribbons add a special touch to your wedding stationery. These can be bought in a set for around £20 in gift shops and department stores.

Stress Busters

- Make a guest list as soon as possible.

- Check the list with both sets of in-laws and invite all close family.

- Find a venue to accommodate guests before finalizing the list.

- Make a reserve list.

- Ask the printer for a proof of the invitation before invitations are printed.

- Check the exact wording, depending on who is hosting the wedding.

- Type or write your invitation out clearly before you arrive at the printers.

- Arrange a collection date well in advance of sending them out.

- Include some useful maps and information for the guests.

- Send invitations at least 8–12 weeks before the wedding.

11 *The Reception*

Throwing a party to celebrate your marriage should be the party of your life; a time to let your hair down, see old friends and revel in all the attention. The average couple spends about £3,717 on the total party package, an increase of £2,174 on 10 years ago. If this seems extravagant, you can throw a great party for a lot less.

The reception venue should reflect the style of your wedding. It could be in a castle, pub, marquee or even at home. Firstly, decide on the size in reference to your guest list, think of costs and take time to look for the perfect venue.

Finding a Venue

Word of mouth is a good way to find out about possible venues. Ask recently married friends and see if they have any suggestions. Go and visit any venue that you are considering and make sure it is right for you – once you have paid your deposit, a venue is unlikely to refund your money just because you have changed your mind.

The options could be a marquee, hotel, restaurant, club, stately home or any other suitable site. If you have a small budget, think about having the reception at home; this can be extremely effective, and with imaginative decoration you can transform your home.

Also, church halls or pub reception rooms are often great value for money. Send off for a list of recently licensed premises for marriage. There's everything from stately homes and film studios to roller coasters and even an old iron-clad battleship. If you're not having a church wedding you could marry and party in the same venue!

Booking Your Venue

Book as early as possible, as popular venues are reserved months in advance. It's important to clarify when you book exactly what purpose you intend to use the venue for, how long you wish to stay and whether music is allowed.

If you are booking a hotel or restaurant it is likely that most of the decoration and catering will be organized by the staff. In which case, make absolutely sure that the price you are quoted includes everything you think it does.

Don't forget to arrange whether you or the venue will organize flowers and other details. Have a formal meeting with the manager, clarify all the details and then ask for a written quote detailing everything that the cost covers. Look over this with a fine-tooth comb before agreeing to it and then ask for written confirmation that you have definitely booked the venue for your wedding date.

Check-list for Choosing a Venue

▮ Availability.

▮ Parking space.

▮ Enough lavatories.

▮ Fairly near to church.

▮ Space for guests.

▌ Cloakroom space (particularly in winter).

▌ A licence for alcohol consumption (if not, apply for a licence from a magistrates' court).

▌ Can they supply food?

▌ Can they supply drink?

▌ Are you allowed to supply your own food and drink and if so how much is corkage?

▌ Are waiting staff available?

▌ Will the venue be suitable if it rains? If not, find out if there is an inside room.

▌ What time will it close?

▌ What exactly does the quote include?

▌ What facilities are there for music?

Catering

The best way to find out about a caterer is by word of mouth. If you can't do that, ask for references and estimates from prospective caterers. Find out the type of food they specialize in and decide whether their cuisine is compatible with what you're looking for.

Write to or telephone the referees and ask them about the quality of the food and service. Contact more than one referee for each company.

Once you are satisfied with the company, be clear about what you want. They will need to know the size of the reception, your budget per head and the date and place of the reception.

If they offer set menus, ask to see a choice and make sure you are happy with all the courses on the menu. Remember to ask for alternative menus for guests with special dietary requirements. Before you agree on anything, ask for a detailed quote. Check that it includes the following in the costs:

- tables and chairs;

- napkins;

- tablecloths;

- crockery;

- cutlery;

- flowers and vases;

- waiting staff;

- clearing up;

- table stationery.

The Wedding Cake

The wedding cake usually acts as a decorative centrepiece at the reception. The once popular custom of crumbling pieces of wedding cake over the bride's head has luckily died out. However, the tradition of the bride and groom making the first cut of the cake as a symbol of a shared future still holds.

The most traditional type is a fruit cake with two to four decorated tiers. Chocolate cakes are now extremely popular. The only advantage of a fruit cake is that if you decide to keep the top layer for your child's christening it will stay fresh.

If you have the cake made by a professional, order it months in advance. Ask to see a specimen album of the types of cakes available. Ask also for a taste sample of the cake you are ordering.

When asking for quotes check that the pillars, display tray and top decorations are provided in the price. For a simple three-tiered cake expect to pay £150 upwards. The delivery of the cake on the day needs to be planned to the last detail. Ensure that each tier will be packed in a separate box.

If you choose to make the cake yourself, you'll make significant savings. A rich fruit cake tastes better when mature. Ideally, start baking three months before the wedding for best results. Ask a competent friend to decorate it for you if you feel intricate cake decoration is beyond your capacities. Wedding magazines offer a good source of inspiration.

Drinks

It is usual to offer pre-meal drinks to your guests before they eat. Traditionally the bride and groom are toasted with champagne. Alternatively, you could offer sparkling wine, sherry, white wine or red wine. If you want to save money, bucks fizz is a good option as the orange juice will cut down on the expense.

If champagne is over your budget, look at the sparkling wine alternatives of which there are some great brands. If you aren't a wine aficionado there are some excellent wine guides available that give you the low-down on inexpensive but quality wines, sparkling wines and champagne. For some expert advice try *The Sunday Telegraph Good Wine Guide*. During the meal, wine is commonly served. A good rule of thumb is to allocate one-half to three-quarters of a bottle of wine per head.

Provide non-alcoholic drinks for children, non-drinkers and drivers during and before the meal. If you can afford it, offer a choice as you'll probably find that even drinkers would like a soft drink at some point in the proceedings. Offering coffee and tea with the cake is also a good idea. Most people need a hot drink to help digest the vast meal they have consumed.

Does Your Venue Have a Drinks Licence?

Check that the reception venue is licensed for the consumption of alcohol. If for some reason it is not, apply for a temporary or occasional licence from the magistrates' court. This can take up to 28 days.

Can Venues Supply Alcoholic Drinks?

Most hotels will supply drinks. Check this sort of detail with the venue before you book. Ask for the exact cost and be precise about the amount of drink required. The catering manager of the hotel should be able to give you advice on wine.

Most hotels or equipped venues will be able to offer you a 'pay bar' or an 'open bar'. In the first instance your guests pay and in the second you pay. According to your budget, you might want to switch to a pay bar at an allocated time to stop your more enthusiastic guests drinking your entire wedding budget.

What About Doing the Drinks Ourselves?

It is usually cheaper to supply your own drink; however, check the price of so-called corkage, which is the charge for opening and serving the wine. Ask the hotel bar or venue about this. If you are doing it yourself, make sure you order the alcohol in plenty of time to ensure it's available in the bulk you require. Remember to think about the food you are offering when choosing the wine to accompany your meal.

When buying in bulk, wine merchants or off-licences will often supply on a sale-or-return basis, which will save you money. Otherwise, any leftovers can make a good start to a wine cellar for your married life.

It's often possible to rent glasses when you purchase the wine. Rent a few extra in case of breakages and build some money into your budget to pay for any smashed glass. Think about the type of glasses you require and if you would like a particular shape for different drinks. If you're not too sure about this, ask your wine merchant who should have a detailed knowledge of such matters.

Order of Ceremonies

Toastmasters

The toastmaster's function at a wedding is as a master of ceremonies. His or her duties can include announcements of the arrival of guests, the start of lunch or supper, the beginning of the toasts and speeches, announcing that the cake will be cut and the 'going away' of the bride and groom. Toastmasters usually cost about £200. They are by no means obligatory and their presence at a wedding is down to personal preference.

Toasts and Speeches

Tradition dictates that the bride's father, the bridegroom and the best man all make a speech, in that order, after the meal at the reception. Keep it brief and short and don't drink too much. Nowadays some brides and chief bridesmaids like to have their say too. If this is the case, do keep speeches to a minimum, more than four and your guests will probably fall asleep. The best man finishes off his speeches by reading out faxes or messages from absent guests.

The Seating Plan

If the reception has a sit-down meal, a seating plan is necessary. Once you have received the final reply and you know the exact numbers, you can start to arrange your seating plan. Some people like to segregate young and old, or put friends and family on different tables. Again this is up to you.

If you can, try to place a couple of people who know each other on the same table. A wedding is a fun place for guests to meet unexpected and interesting characters. Everyone is usually in good spirits, so think about your seating plan carefully and try to seat guests next to someone they are likely to get on with.

The convention is that as far as possible men and women should sit next to each other. Place cards help to avoid confusion and should be written by hand in ink pen.

The Top Table

The bridal couple sit with their families at the top table. The usual seating plan from left to right is:

- chief bridesmaid;

- groom's father;

- bride's mother;

- groom;

- bride;

▌ bride's father;

▌ groom's mother;

▌ best man.

The Receiving Line

The receiving line is made up of the hosts and members of the bridal party. A receiving line allows guests to congratulate the bride and groom and their families. This is a particularly good idea if it's a big wedding as otherwise some guests might not find an opportunity to speak to the bride or groom.

If you are having a toastmaster he or she will introduce guests. Guests will usually pass along the receiving line on their way to their table or to the buffet.

The standard order of the receiving line for a Christian wedding is:

▌ the bride's mother;

▌ the groom's father;

▌ the groom's mother;

▌ the bride's father;

▌ the bride;

▌ the groom;

▌ the chief bridesmaid;

▌ the best man.

The standard order of the receiving line for a Jewish wedding is:

- the bride's mother;

- the bride's father;

- the bride;

- the groom;

- the groom's mother;

- the groom's father.

There is no reason to stick rigidly to tradition and if you prefer it is possible simply to have the bride and groom in the receiving line.

Music

See Chapter 13: Wedding Ceremony and Reception Music.

Stress Busters

- Book the reception venue as far in advance as possible.

- Check the venue has facilities for music.

- Make sure you have a written quote detailing exactly what you are paying for.

- Check what time the venue closes.

- Book the caterer as far in advance as possible.

- Decide whether you or the venue will supply the drinks.

- Check the price of corkage.

12 *The Ceremony*

For many people the wedding ceremony is a daunting ordeal. The idea of following legal and social rituals in public often leads to pre-wedding jitters. Don't worry, in most cases the bride and groom have a major input into how they would like to wed. The key is to discuss it thoroughly with your registrar or minister so you know exactly what to expect on the day.

Civil Ceremonies

Since 1997 couples marrying in a civil wedding can choose a more modern declaration of vows. Have a meeting with your registrar before you wed to choose your vows. At this point you can also discuss the order of service, which is flexible in a civil marriage, and any additions like poetry and non-religious music.

Religious Ceremonies

Speak to your minister about the order of service and specifications for your wedding service. For example, in Church of England weddings, one of the main things to decide is whether you want to use traditional or non-traditional language. A traditional ceremony would use the 1928 Series One version of the Book of Common Prayer. For a more modern ceremony the Alternative Service Book is the one to choose. An updated version, the new Book of Common Worship, harks back to a more traditional set of marriage vows and will be available from the end of 1999. There is no need for the bride to promise to 'obey' any more; this is now an optional part of the wedding vows.

For Roman Catholic ceremonies the choice is between having a ceremony within mass or outside mass. For Jewish weddings the type of ceremony will be dictated by whether you are marrying within the orthodox, reform or liberal tradition – or not. Couples-to-be should contact their local rabbi to discuss the possibilities for their wedding ceremony. Many faiths allow some kind of personalization of the marriage vows. This should always be discussed before the ceremony.

Readings and Prayers

In religious ceremonies, readings and prayers allow you to add a personal touch to your wedding. You could even write your own prayers. All choices have to be approved by your minister. Your minister will have a wealth of ideas to help you but for some extra inspiration, below are some wedding-related Bible readings you could consider using extracts from.

King James Version:

Ecclesiastes 4: 9–12
Two are better than one because they have a good reward for their labour.

Genesis 2: 20–25
The creation of woman.

John 4: 7–12
Beloved let us love one another for love is of God.

Ruth 1: 16–17... for wither thou goest, I will go; and where thou lodgest, I will lodge: thy people shall be my people, and thy God my God.

The Song of Solomon 2: 10–13
My beloved spake, and said unto me,
Rise up my love, my fair one, and come away.

The Song of Solomon 8: 6–7
Set me a seal upon thine arm: for love is strong as death.

For more inspiration for readings and prayers for your wedding there is an excellent Web site packed with relevant information. Check it out online at www.weddings.co.uk

Music

See the chapter on music.

Signing the Register

The register is signed by the person performing the marriage, the bride and groom and two chosen witnesses. The bride uses her maiden name. The bride and groom follow the minister to the vestry to sign the register. The bride's mother follows on the arm of the groom's father, behind them are the groom's mother and the bride's father followed by the chief bridesmaid and the best man or any other adult attendants.

The Usual Format of a Church Wedding

The wedding march starts and the groom and the best man rise from their seats at the front of the church and move to

83

the top of the aisle. The minister stands at the front of the church.

The bride walks down the aisle on her father's right, so when she reaches the end of the aisle she is in the right position to take her marriage vows – on her husband's left.

Usually the groom and the best man turn to greet the bride and the chief bridesmaid now takes her bouquet and lifts her veil. At this point the minister will greet everyone present and then a hymn is sung as a prelude to the marriage.

The minister gives a general introduction to the wedding. He or she asks who is giving away the bride. The bride's father either nods or steps forward. He then takes the bride's hand and offers it palm down to the minister.

The minister places the bride's hand in the groom's right hand. The bride's father now sits down. The minister guides the couple through the marriage vows. Once vows and rings have been exchanged, the minister declares the couple legally married.

Rehearsal

For most church weddings a rehearsal is necessary one week in advance. Make sure that the entire wedding party knows when the rehearsal is and can attend. This should take some of the nerves out of the big day.

Common Order of Arrival

The ushers normally arrive about 45–60 minutes before the service in order to be ready to greet guests. They should be ready with the orders of service to hand out to each guest before ushering them to their seats.

The organist arrives about 30 minutes early to start playing the organ to accompany guests as they enter the church.

The minister arrives about 20 minutes before the service.

The groom and best man arrive about 20 minutes before the service.

Most guests will arrive about 15 minutes before the service begins.

The bride's mother arrives about 10 minutes before the service is about to begin. One of the ushers escorts her to her seat.

The bride and her father will, of course, arrive last. This should be within a few minutes of the start time of the wedding.

Seating

The first one or two pews are normally reserved for the couple's immediate families, the second one or two for more distant relations and the pews behind that are for friends.

The bride's mother sits in the front pew on the left of the aisle. The bride's family traditionally sit on the left behind the bride and the groom's family on the right behind the groom.

Ushers should seat any latecomers at the back of the church, making as little noise as possible.

13 Wedding Ceremony and Reception Music

Music is an essential part of the ceremony and celebrations for most people. For a civil wedding the choice is up to you, as long as you choose non-religious music. At a religious wedding the choice will to some extent depend on your faith.

The general rule is that Roman Catholic ceremonies only allow music with a religious dimension, whereas for a Church of England or a Church of Wales ceremony classical or popular music is allowed. Quaker weddings never feature music. In a church wedding the priest or vicar customarily approves which hymns and pieces of music are chosen.

Music in the Church

Example Order of Service

▋ The Procession (with music)

▋ Introduction

▋ Hymn

▋ The Lesson and Reading

▋ The Marriage

▌ The Prayers

▌ Hymn

▌ The Blessing

▌ The Signing of the Register (with music)

▌ The Recession (with music)

Which Hymns Shall We Choose?

Generally there are two to three hymns sung at a church wedding. One before the service, one after the marriage and the final hymn after the couple have signed the register.

There are no strict rules and you can have as many as you like – but remember not to make the ceremony too long.

Think about the position of the hymn in the service. The first hymn sung at the beginning of the service is customarily in praise of God, whereas the second sung after the union of the bride and groom is a celebration of the marriage.

If you are not a regular churchgoer you may need some help. Your vicar will be a great source of advice. (See also the list of popular wedding hymns later in this chapter.)

What About Music to Accompany the Hymns?

It's a good idea to choose traditional tunes of hymns so that the majority of your congregation can sing heartily. If a choir is available they liven up the proceedings and encourage any nervous singers. You'll need to negotiate a price and check that the choir is free on the date of your wedding. If not, you could hire a professional choir; however, this could be pricey.

An organ accompanying the hymns is usually possible for an additional fee. Talk to the organist and choirmaster and decide on music; they will know what is suitable and possible. However, don't be bullied, it's your wedding so the final decision is up to you.

What About Other Music?

You could hire some professional musicians to play a classical or popular piece during the ceremony. A professional singer can make a stunning addition to the musical content of the ceremony.

Do discuss this with your minister as it is up to him or her to decide what he or she deems fit for a religious marriage ceremony. If musicians are to be paid on the day then traditionally the responsibility falls to the best man.

Bells

A glorious peal of bells when leaving the church can be arranged for about £30 to £60. Check that bell-ringers are available on your wedding day.

How Shall We Arrange Our Order-of-service Sheets?

The name of the hymn and the composer should be on the order-of-service sheets. Hymns can be written out in full on the order-of-service sheet and this is probably the simplest way.

Be careful about issues of copyright. Copyright holders are usually listed in a printed hymn book and should be contacted before reproducing any words. They will require either a small fee or a printed acknowledgement.

Popular Wedding Hymns (with some suggestions from The Royal School of Church Music)

All People that on Earth do Dwell
All that I Am

Amazing Grace
And Can it Be that I should Gain
And Did Those Feet in Ancient Time
At the Name of Jesus
Be Thou My Vision
Bind Us Together
Christ Triumphant Ever Reigning
Come Down O Love Divine
Dear Lord and Father of Mankind
Father Hear the Prayer We Offer
For the Beauty of the Earth
God of All Living
Great Is Thy Faithfulness
Guide Me O Thou Great Redeemer
How Great Thou Art
I Vow to Thee My Country
Immortal Invisible God Only Wise
Lead Us Heavenly Father Lead Us
Let There be Love Shared Among Us
Lord of All Hopefulness
Lord for the Years
Love Divine All Love Excelling
Make Me a Channel of Your Peace
May the Grace of Christ Our Saviour
Now Thank We All Our God
O God of Love to Thee We Bow
O Jesus I Have Promised
O Perfect Love
O Praise Ye the Lord
O Worship the King
Praise My Soul the King of Heaven
Take My Life and Let It Be
The Grace of Life is Theirs
The King of Love my Shepherd Is
The Lord's My Shepherd I'll Not Want

To God Be the Glory
What a Friend We Have in Jesus
You Shall Go Out With Joy

For a great guide to hymns (with music supplied for some)
check out www.weddingguide.co.uk

Top Tips for Classical Wedding Favourites (with some suggestions from The Royal School of Church Music)

Before

Haydn	Eight Pieces for Musical Clocks
Bach	Movements from Trio Sonatas
Bossi	Scherzo in G minor

Bride's entrance

Bliss	A Wedding Fanfare
Mozart	Wedding March – Marriage of Figaro
Purcell	Fanfare
Handel	Arrival of the Queen of Sheba
Saint-Saens	Charole-Fanfare from 3rd Symphony
Ives	Intrada

Register signing

Bach	Air on the G String
Bach	Ave Maria
Bach	Jesu, Joy of Man's Desiring
Rutter	Toccata in Seven
Walton	Touch her soft lips (from Henry V)
Rheinberger	Cantilena from 11th Sonata

Bride and groom exit

Elgar	Pomp & Circumstance March No. 4
Hollins	Bridal March
Mendelssohn	Wedding March – Midsummer Night's Dream
Wagner	Wedding March – Lohengrin
Mathias	Processional
Smart	Festive March in D

Anthems and vocal music

A Wedding Blessing	Brown
Blessing	Ridout
My Beloved Spake	Hadley
God be Merciful	Gant

Music at a Civil Ceremony

For civil ceremonies you are less restricted in your choice. However, a register office will not permit the use of religious music.

Find out if your venue has facilities like a stereo and speakers to play your chosen tapes or CDs. If you want to hire professional musicians, think about the size of your venue.

Music at the Reception

This is the time for everyone to let their hair down. Depending on your inclination you can choose anything from a ceilidh to some thumping funky beats. A wedding is an opportunity for everyone to take part. So think about the age range of your guests and choose music that can be enjoyed by all.

Stress Busters

Check that your wedding and reception venues have adequate facilities for music.

Think about music appropriate for the size of your venue.

Use musicians that you have heard or have been recommended.

Book musicians as much in advance as possible.

For a church wedding discuss your choice of music with your minister.

Check the availability of bell-ringers, choir and organist.

Choose hymns in relation to their order in the ceremony.

14 The Bride's Clothes

On her wedding day every bride wants to look her best. The average bride spends £860 on her dress, £435 on her attendants' outfits and £136 on her going away outfit – a total of £1,431.

The bride's outfit is likely to be one of your major wedding expenses. Getting the dress right can cause more anxiety than any other detail of the wedding. But, it doesn't have to be hell, it can be great fun.

This chapter takes the stress out of shopping around for the perfect outfit and gives loads of helpful tips on how to find the ideal dress for each bride to complement her individual wedding.

The Dress

The Search for Inspiration

There are loads of bride's magazines with seasonal and up-to-date ideas for brides and bridesmaids. Go to your local newsagent and buy a range of wedding titles and you will soon become familiar with what's on the market.

Try to narrow down what you are looking for by considering the type of ceremony you are having and the style of dress that would be most appropriate. A grand church wedding requires a long off-white or white dress. In civil weddings there is no rule, a long white dress or smart suit is equally appropriate.

For inspiration, start a wedding dress file. Cut out pictures of styles or parts of styles you like. You could even add a picture of your wedding venue so you can be inspired by your wedding surroundings.

The Type of Dress

By looking through bride's magazines you should be able to find out what's in for the season. Or you might decide to plump for something more traditional.

Remember your figure shape. If you are on the small side, avoid the multi-layered skirt effect as you may end up looking spherical. Draw attention to your best features and cover up your worst.

Think about the back of your dress because that will be the view that most people see during the ceremony.

Consider the season of the wedding. For late spring or summer weddings, light fabrics are common, like cool silk, chiffon, cotton or lace. For late autumn and winter, heavier fabrics like velvet, brocade and duchess satin are more common.

According to *Wedding and Home* magazine, between 1988 and 1989 there was a 20 per cent increase in the number of brides who choose to wear white at their wedding. Pure white is usually better for brunettes, while ivory or cream is more flattering for blondes and redheads. Mature brides or those marrying for the second time around should think of near-white colours.

Now you have a starting point to work from. The next step is where to get your dress.

Where to Get Your Dress

There is a range of different options available to you.

Valencia Style BC20716 £650

A specialist wedding store or department store

Off-the-peg dresses start in the range of about £195. There are some stunning dresses now available from companies like Pronuptia and Virgin Bride. Usually appointments must be made to try anything on. Telephone retailers beforehand if you want to do more than just look. Even an off-the-peg dress can take up to eight weeks before it's ready. So, give yourself time. Most stores will do alterations. Again, bridal magazines are packed with advertisements for designers, retailers and couture wedding suppliers. The real advantage of buying a new dress from a specialist store is that you'll often be able to buy all the accessories and the dress in the same place.

A second-hand wedding dress agency

There are many agencies that can find once-worn designer dresses at a reasonable price. Look in the back of wedding magazines for advertisements. They can try to find an exact make and style in your size or you can browse through their stocks to see if anything catches your eye. Normally the agency will subsequently fit the dress to your exact size. Unlike hiring, because you own the dress, you can make as few or as many alterations as you desire. This sometimes works out as a very economic way of buying your dress and you can end up with a glamorous designer dress like a Jasper Conran for about half the price. Most agencies will also offer second-hand dresses from the cheaper end of the market. If you don't mind a dress that's about two years old, you can pick up a real bargain.

Have a one-off made

To be the one and only, you could consider having your dress designed for you. If you've got bags of money, a one-off from

"...and they look so good together."

anello & davide

HAND MADE BRIDAL SHOES

47 Beauchamp Place, Chelsea, London SW3 1NX. Tel 0171 225 2468 Fax 0171 225 2111
E-mail info@anellodavide.co.uk

a specialist designer is the thing. Alternatively, you could find a design you like and approach a dressmaker who might be able to do something for you at a better price. Unless you're a brilliant dressmaker it's inadvisable to do it yourself. The hassle may prove too much during the run-up to your wedding. If you decide to make your own dress, ensure you get the best deal when buying the material. Shop around as prices vary enormously. If you can't visit the shop in person, ask to be sent swatches before you make your final decision.

Borrow or hire a dress

If you don't want to keep your dress after the wedding, hiring is a good option. Hiring normally costs about £300. But, don't leave it to the last minute. Even hiring a dress, you'll need to order it at least 12 weeks beforehand. The dress will normally be ready to collect two days before the wedding. For something to make you feel a million dollars, Angels and Bermans (0171 836 5678) guarantee a wedding to 'fulfil your most star-struck fantasy'. You could rent Andie MacDowell's dress from *Four Weddings and a Funeral* and into the bargain, hire a costume for the groom and marry your own Mr Darcy. Of course, you'll have to find a star's costume that is the correct size. Angels and Bermans' wedding dress rental ranges from £150 to £450. Other costumes can be hired for about £60.

Don't rule out borrowing. It might even be lucky. Ask your mother and grandmother to unearth their dresses from the attic. You never know, one might be the perfect fit! Or perhaps a friend of yours has married recently and would be happy for you to borrow hers. Make sure you are allowed to make minor alterations.

Trying On the Dress

▌ Be adventurous, you don't know until you've tried. Try dresses that you don't instantly fall in love with on the hanger.

▌ Take hairclips or a hairband so you can try on the dress with your hair up.

▌ Wear white or light-coloured underwear that fits you well.

▌ Bring at least two people with you so they can see you from every angle.

▌ Try not to book more than three or four appointments a day or you'll become jaded and it will stop being fun.

Accessories

Shoes

Start looking for shoes as soon as you've decided on the dress. You'll need to know the height of your heels in order to finalize the length of your hem.

Bring a swatch with you when you go shoe shopping to compare colour and texture. Detail is important when you want to look perfect. You can ask for a sample of your wedding dress when you order.

Although strappy sandals can look feminine, don't get stuck with your toes out in the middle of January. Apart from looking ridiculous you'll also be freezing. So think about the season in which you are marrying.

Also, remember comfort! You'll have to wear the shoes for a good few hours. To avoid your feet swelling, or worse, falling flat on your face at the reception, try to find a medium-sized heel.

If you can't find the exact colour of shoe you want, you can always have them dyed. This is also a great way of matching up shoes for bridesmaids. Allow about three weeks for professional dying. Some retailers will do this themselves and it should cost in the region of £40.

Veils

Veils are an optional part of your wedding outfit. They can have one, two or three layers depending on how thick you would like your veil to look.

Another decision will be the style of veil. 'Church' is a full-length veil that ends about a foot beyond the dress, 'Cathedral' will be about six feet longer than the train, 'Fingertip' will end where your fingertips touch the dress and 'Mantilla' is a lace-trimmed one-layer veil that frames your face.

An antique veil can be stunning and they are softer than some modern veils, particularly those made of man-made fibres. Antique veils range from £200 to £2,000. A good contact for antique veils is the Honiton Lace Shop in Honiton, Devon (tel: 01404 42416).

Lingerie

Take your bridesmaid with you and have some fun shopping for beautiful, sexy underwear that makes you feel like a princess. Ideally it should fit snugly and be in the correct shade so it is not visible through the wedding outfit. This usually means white or cream.

Your wedding day is a good opportunity to wear something different. If you are normally quite conservative, go for the whole shebang, including suspenders, stockings and matching separates in silk, lace and satin.

If you are on a budget, an all-in-one 'body' can work out cheaper. For lingerie stockists, look at the numerous advertisements in the back of bridal magazines. Marks & Spencer is still one of the best deals for quality underwear at reasonable prices. Or splash out on luxury designer names like Janet Reger or even Rigby and Peller who are famous for their fitted hand-made bras.

Headdress

For the final touch you can decorate your hair with a head-dress of flowers (see the chapter on flowers). If you decide on jewellery, choose a wedding tiara or crown that matches your dress, veil and colouring.

You could choose coloured stones to add a delicate touch to your bridal tiara. If possible choose gemstones to reflect the colour of your eyes.

Going Away Outfit

Once you've sorted out clothes for the ceremony and reception, you can start thinking about the going away outfit. Usually the going away outfit is something smart and stylish.

If you are going on honeymoon immediately after the wedding you'll have to find something right for travelling and for the climate to which you are going. A good idea is to choose a thin dress with a top and jacket. You can then remove layers as you heat up or add socks and a jumper to keep you warm on the plane.

Bridesmaids

Once you have picked your bridesmaids, your next decision is to work out what they should wear. Do wait until you have chosen your dress as it is important that the bridesmaids' outfits tone with what you are wearing. Modern bridesmaids do not have to look identical. This is a useful tip if your bridesmaids are completely different shapes, sizes and even ages. However, do choose a theme, like a colour or style, to give a sense of uniformity. It can be effective to reflect details in the outfits – all the bridesmaids might have the same hairstyle or shoes, for example.

Have a meeting with the bridesmaids to discuss the overall look. Make it clear in the meeting whether you want to help the bridesmaids choose their outfits or if you are happy for them to do it themselves. This will avoid any misunderstandings. For a harmonious appearance it is usually much better if the bride has the final say. However, if you are asking the bridesmaids to pay for their outfits, it is only reasonable to agree on outfits that your bridesmaids can wear again.

Stress Busters

▍ Give yourself a fixed budget for the dress.

▍ Buy lots of bride's magazines and get an idea of the range available – keep a wedding dress file so you know what you want.

▍ If you are on a budget, think about hiring or buying second hand.

▍ Remember your rear view will be the most important one in the church.

▍ Choose shoes as soon as possible so the hemline of your dress can be adjusted.

▍ When trying on the dress, bring a hair band to put your hair up.

15 *The Groom's Clothes*

The average British groom spends about £350 on his wedding outfit – which is under half of what the average bride spends on her attire. The groom might spend less, but it's just as important for him to look right on the big day.

Finding the perfect wedding wear should be done at least three months in advance, allowing time to shop around and have any alterations done. Whatever the choice, it must fit properly. The key is to get measured correctly and have as many fittings as are necessary.

Although it's still traditional for the groom to be kept in the dark about his bride's outfit, you can reach a joint decision on the basics. For example, discuss whether your style will be formal or informal and perhaps on a general colour scheme. The chief bridesmaid can also be a great help to the groom. He should remember to check with her before making any daring buys – that wild fuchsia cravat might seem like a good idea but first make sure you won't clash with the bride.

Choosing What to Wear

The Morning Suit

There is no real formal rule for weddings as it is a personal celebration. A black morning suit is the most traditional garb for a groom and is commonly worn at church weddings. For formal weddings this is usually worn with striped trousers and a buff or grey waistcoat.

Other Options

Have fun with what you wear, this is a joyous occasion. Nowadays, there is a wonderful variety of styles available to the groom. From lounge suits and frock coats to Nehru-style jackets or even kilts, you can choose a style that suits your wedding, your bride's dress and you.

Dinner Suits

Dinner suits and black ties are not common at British weddings; however, they are popular for weddings in the United States and abroad.

Finding an Outfit

There are basically four options available to you. You can either buy something new, have a 'bespoke' or a 'made to measure' suit made, or hire. You might even want to mix and match – buy a shirt, some trousers and shoes and hire the rest.

Buying a Suit Off The Peg

A ready-made suit in a standard size will cost around £200. There are some brilliant wedding menswear ranges available across the UK. Pronuptia offers everything from morning suits and lounge suits to evening wear and kilts.

The great thing about the big chains like Pronuptia and Virgin Bride is that they offer a one-stop service as they can supply you with all the accessories like hats, handkerchiefs, cuff-links and cravats.

However, you'll need to start shopping well in advance to ensure you have a wide choice in your size and leave time for alterations.

A GUIDE TO GETTING MARRIED

When organising your Wedding Stationary it is important to select the correct invitations which will co-ordinate with the style of your wedding. The look of stationery will set the style of your wedding and will tell people what type of person you are.

Making the choice can prove very difficult as there are so many designs to choose from in the market today. Bride & Groom Wedding Service is a mail order catalogue which allows you to sit in the comfort of your own home to make that important decision. Our catalogue offers a wide range of stationery to suit all tastes from cute, traditional to contemporary all at a price that is affordable.

We offer a wide variety of ink colours for added style and elegance, along with a range of type/styles and wording choices. All invitations have matching order of service, menus, reply cards, thank you cards to allow you to coordinate your stationery.

To add that finishing touch to your day we also offer a wide range of accessories that can be personalised with your names and wedding date if requested. The range includes: Personalised serviettes, cakes boxes match books, personalised champagne flutes, guest books and so much more.

Bride and Groom Wedding Service is the UKs leading Mail Order Wedding Stationery Catalogue. We pride ourselves on producing high quality products and offer a fast efficient delivery service. We have a team of highly trained customer service staff who are available to provide information and advise on all products to make ordering easy and to ensure that you make the right decision.

Bride & Groom Wedding Service offers a 30 day money back guarantee with every item shown in our catalogue. If you are unsatisfied with any product purchased from us, simply return it postage paid within 30 days of receipt for a full refund.

*Should you require further information on our products or would like to request our **FREE 72 page full colour brochure** please contact us on our Freephone number: 0500 006573 where someone will be happy to assist you.*

Look in the back of wedding magazines for menswear retailers.

Hiring

This is a great option if you're not likely to wear your outfit again. It can work out extremely cheaply – anywhere upwards of about £50 for the whole shebang.

Most hirers will be able to supply you with accessories like a hat, shirt, gloves and ties as well. In Austin Reed in London a fancy waistcoat costs around £11 and a morning suit £39.95.

Don't think you can just run in the day before you wed and slip into an ideal outfit; it is advisable to book a hired suit two to three months in advance to ensure your size is available.

Of the many hire shops available, Moss Bros is probably the most famous but many major gentlemen's outfitters have hire departments in selected branches.

Look in your local Yellow Pages or in the advertisement section at the back of wedding magazines for hire shops.

Ordering a Bespoke Suit

If you want something extremely special for your wedding day, a bespoke suit is the thing. It is made by hand and entails numerous fittings to cut the suit to your exact specifications. You choose the style, size and fabric that you want.

The garment is hand cut and built on the body by the tailor and the fitter. At each fitting stage the tailor re-assesses the body fit and any additional requirements that the customer might require.

Such personal service doesn't come cheap. Prices start at around £800 and go up and up.

Having a Suit Made to Measure

A suit specialist like Austin Reed will have a made-to-measure department in most of their stores. A made-to-measure suit is also chosen from a range of fabrics and styles and tailored to your body shape. Made to measure is cheaper than a bespoke suit because it is cut in a factory and there is only one fitting. It will set you back between £400 and £650.

Firstly, a customer has his measurements taken, and then an in-depth consultation in which he chooses the style, type of cloth and any extras like pockets. When the suit is ready, if the customer has slightly gained or lost weight, alterations will be made. Such alterations should be free of charge.

Stress Busters

▌ Buy a load of wedding magazines for ideas on what's available.

▌ Start looking at least three months in advance – even if you're hiring or buying off the peg.

▌ Bring along a friend for advice when you shop – this is where the best man comes in handy.

▌ Have yourself measured before you try on anything.

▌ Don't clash with the bride; tell the chief bridesmaid what you're planning to wear before you pay for anything.

▌ Make sure your trousers are the right length and that the sleeves of your jacket allow for an inch of the shirt cuff to be seen.

▌ Don't buy anything tight fitting, it won't look good and it will spoil your pleasure at the reception.

▌ Buy your wedding shoes at least a month before the wedding and wear them in the house to stop you getting blisters on your big day.

▌ Make sure your best man and the ushers co-ordinate their clothes with yours.

16 The Wedding Ring

Incredibly, most couples spend more on flowers for their wedding day than they do on a wedding ring that will last a lifetime. A recent survey conducted for *Wedding and Home* magazine discovered that the average groom spends £228 on his bride's ring while flowers for the day cost about £247.

According to the same survey, 98 per cent of brides now buy a ring for their groom at an average cost of £208. In a Church of England ceremony it is obligatory for the bride to be given a ring.

In most other forms of service the ring exchange is a standard part of the wedding ceremony, not a compulsory one. For the superstitious, beware, wearing a ring before the ceremony (which doesn't include trying it on!) could bring bad luck to the marriage.

The Classic Wedding Ring

The classic wedding ring is a plain band made of gold. In recent years, platinum rings have become popular, as have more decorative rings; they now account for about 40 per cent of the market.

Mixed metal bands are fashionable this season. Texture is the key. Two-tone rings can be made of a mixture of gold and platinum or a combination of hues of gold, for example contrast white gold with yellow gold. Also popular are tiny diamond studs in the band. This design looks particularly effective with white gold and platinum.

For a touch of royal flair, have your wedding ring made out of Welsh gold. Favoured by the Royal family for their wedding rings, Welsh gold is rare, and has a special collectors' interest because it is mined in the British Isles.

Because more couples than ever before cohabit before they marry, some do not enter into a formal engagement and so buy a wedding and engagement ring in one. If this is the case the wedding ring is likely to include a gemstone.

Where to Get Your Ring

▌ Contact the National Association of Goldsmiths for a list of their members in your area (tel: 0845 604 0165).

▌ Compare quality and prices. At the top end of the market, Asprey and Garrard offer traditional wedding bands ranging from a gold band for £320 to a platinum band for £500. A diamond-set gold band is £560 and a platinum one £795. Whereas in Beaverbrooks, an 18 carat plain gold wedding band starts at £99.50 and goes up to about £325.

▌ Most good quality retailers will make up something to your design. But be careful – your design might not work as well as you think. It's usually better to go to a professional designer.

▌ If you would like your ring designed for you, contact the British Jewellers Association on 0121 236 2657. They keep an updated database of designers who are backed by the association.

▌ Visit some design fairs to get ideas. Every September, the Goldsmith's Fair is packed with designers often showing innovative and beautiful designs. Contact 0171 606 7010.

If you live near Birmingham, visit Hockley where the Jewellery Quarter is literally packed with small workshops and discount jewellery outlets. Every price range is catered for here. Another famous jewellery area is around the Hatton Garden area of London in Clerkenwell. Similarly, the area is full of workshops where jewellery is made on site.

Choosing Your Ring

All jewellers will have a device to measure your finger. The chosen ring will be made to your size specifications unless they have your size in stock. When you are supplied with the ring, make sure you are happy with the fit.

Choose your wedding ring with your engagement ring in mind. For a start they have to match as you will be wearing them on the same finger for the rest of your life. Consider the type of metals used in both rings. Platinum is harder than 22 carat gold, and can wear a gold ring down when they are worn together over a long period of time.

If you are choosing rings for the bride and groom, perhaps think of ways to match the rings, in shape, type of metal or perhaps even in small details on the ring.

Materials

Gold

Because pure gold is so soft it is mixed with other metals to make it stronger. This is where the 'carat' comes in. The higher the carat the purer the gold. Top of the range is 22 carat gold because it's the purest and most expensive. However, it's also the least strong. 18 carat and 9 carat are cheaper and less pure but stronger. Gold has a range of hues from yellow to a rosy gold.

Platinum

Platinum jewellery is made from pure platinum because it is a stronger metal than gold.

Silver

Silver is cheaper than platinum and gold. However, over many years it will show scratches and become thinner.

Stress Busters

- Choose the wedding ring together.

- Choose extremely carefully as your wedding ring is for life.

- When choosing, think of your engagement ring.

- Set a budget first.

- Go to some design fairs to get ideas.

- Have it fitted correctly.

17 Transport – Getting to the Church on Time

Basic transport hire costs around £150 upwards and the average UK couple spend about £249 on their wedding transport. All eyes will be on your transport when it arrives at the wedding venue, so be prepared to make an entrance.

Anything goes – from the movie-star glitz of a Rolls-Royce or stretch limo to a horse and carriage, American Cadillac or for the more eccentric or country-minded bride, it has even been known for the bride to arrive on a tractor.

What Transport Is Necessary?

For a large wedding there are usually two wedding cars. Traditional wedding etiquette dictates that the first car takes the bride's mother and bridesmaids to the church and then the parents and attendants to the reception. The second car takes the bride and her father to the wedding venue and afterwards the bride and groom to the reception.

The best man is responsible for getting the groom to the church on time. The 'going away' car is also his responsibility.

What Type of Transport?

Coach and Horses

A coach and horses can make any bride feel like a real-life Cinderella. Book early as some popular summer dates are booked up as far as two years in advance. Expect to pay between £400 and £800.

Car Hire

One of the most popular options is to approach a reputable car hire company. Either contact a recommended company, look in the Yellow Pages for addresses or check out the Internet where there are lists of car companies, often advertised by region. With so many different types to choose from, here's our list of some popular types of wedding car.

Modern

From the 1970s onwards, including the famous Rolls-Royce Silver Spirit or Silver Shadow.

Classic

Post-war, at least 20 years old, like a Bentley S1 or a Mark II Jaguar as driven by Inspector Morse.

Pre-war

Any car post-1931 and pre-1940.

A vintage car up to 1931

A vintage car is one made between 1917 and 1930. Older veteran cars are divided into two sections, those made before 1916 and those made before 1905.

American

American cars are usually 1950s models, including the '59 Cadillac or the modern alternative, the movie star-style stretch limousine.

Car Hire Contacts

If you're looking for something really distinctive, here are some great contacts:

▌ American 50s Car Hire – Pink and white convertibles from 1959 and 1960. Prices start at £175. Contact: 01268 735 914.

▌ Bespoke Chauffeur Hire Specialists – classy cars, including Jaguars and self-drive sports cars. Contact: 01923 250 250.

▌ Cars of Character – a choice of 1,000 cars nationwide. Contact: 01494 792013.

Whichever model you choose, perform the following checks.

Car Hire Company Checks

▌ Visit the company in person.

▌ Clarify that the car you are shown is the actual car used on the day.

▌ Check over the paintwork and the tyres, look for rust and check the interior and upholstery.

▌ Check that all 'extras' are included in the price – chauffeur, decorations, etc.

▌ Practise getting in and out of the car, think about the size of the wedding dress, etc.

▌ Think carefully about the colour of your vehicle – make sure it doesn't clash with your beautifully chosen wedding outfits.

▌ Have everything confirmed in writing.

Parking Arrangements

You will need to find out about parking arrangements for the wedding venue and for the reception. Don't forget this, especially if you're getting wed in town. This is also applicable for your guests. If there is no parking immediately outside your venue, you should make guests aware of this and possibly send parking advice out with the wedding invitations.

Budget Ideas

If you are on a tight budget you could borrow a car or use your own. However, ask a friend to drive it, as you might be too nervous to drive on the day. Most hire companies offer a choice of hire with or without chauffeur. Depending on your budget, you could ask a friend to stand in as chauffeur as an alternative wedding gift.

Stress Busters

▌ Book any transport well in advance to ensure availability.

▌ Follow our check-list when choosing transport.

- Find out about parking space at the reception and the church.

- Make sure you have written confirmation of your quote and the date and time you will need the transport.

- Remember to find the right size of transport – a Robin Reliant and a vast wedding dress don't mix.

18 Flowers at Your Wedding

Flowers for your wedding usually include personal flowers for the wedding party and decorations for the wedding and reception venue. Traditionally, flowers for the wedding party are paid for by the groom, while those for the wedding and reception are paid for by the bride's family. The average UK couple spend £247 on their wedding flowers.

Flowers for your wedding party can include the bride's bouquet and possibly headdress, bridesmaids' bouquets, mothers' corsages and buttonholes for the groom, best man, fathers and ushers. It is also a much-appreciated gesture if the groom gives his mother and mother-in-law small bouquets at the reception.

Choosing the Florist

When choosing a florist, as usual, shop around for the best deals and follow up any personal recommendations. The florist should be given *at least* four months' warning to ensure that he or she is free on the day.

If your budget is tight, try to find a good florist near the church and reception to cut down on delivery costs, and into the bargain you'll make absolutely sure that your flowers are fresh.

Drop in to the shop in person and if you like the look of the flowers, arrange a meeting with the florist. If possible, try to avoid Saturday as they are likely to be very busy.

Photographs or sketches of the interior of the wedding venue, reception venue and the bride's and attendants' dresses will help the florist design arrangements that complement your day.

Be wary of a florist who shows you photos of standard bouquets and isn't able to be flexible.

Flowers for the Wedding Venue and Reception

In a church, the areas to consider are the altar, pulpit, lectern, windowsills, font, columns, church entrance, chancel steps and pew ends.

In a reception venue the flowers may be arranged for you as part of the deal. If not, go and visit the reception area and look for the prominent features in the room. A couple of dramatic arrangements will probably be enough for the main decorations.

As well as this, you could consider decorating the entrance to your reception venue; decorations as guests walk in are a welcoming sight and they can smell wonderful too. Flower arrangements on tables are extremely effective, but ensure they are not too high for guests to see each other!

Flowers for the Bride and Attendants

Unless you are a brilliant flower arranger, the best option is to ask the florist to arrange the flowers for you. This is particularly true of the bridal bouquet and headdress.

Most brides carry a bouquet on their wedding day. Only some choose to wear a headdress. A good florist should be able to work with you and find styles completely suited to your needs.

Bring along some fabrics and even sketches to give an idea of the bride's and attendants' clothes.

Choosing a smaller and simpler version of the bride's bouquet for the attendants is an effective way of harmonizing the aesthetics of the bridal group. The attendants' headdresses (if required) can be similar too, but should always be simpler than the bride's headdress.

Types of Posy

For a delicious traditional-smelling posy, try spray roses. These roses have several flower heads per stem and look particularly delicate. They are small, so easier to hold, and mix readily with other flowers. Freesias are always popular because of their glorious smell and vibrant colours. For brides who desire a monochrome look, it's possible to make a posy purely of white and cream freesias.

For a more classical arrangement, spray roses and freesias mix well with the heady aroma of oriental lilies, pink nerines (a favourite of Lily Langtry) and maroon leucodendron foliage. For winter and spring brides, it's possible to include stems of glossy tulips.

For an old-fashioned English rose posy, try a hand-tied posy of sweet peas, late-season tulips, lisianthus, blowzy peonies, love-in-a-mist, astrantia and trailing variegated ivy as a complement to the roses.

If you prefer a variation on the traditional posy, lily of the valley is readily available in May and has limited availability all the year round. It makes a beautiful arrangement with spray roses, satin-petalled lisanthus, delicately spotted alstremeria, and hypericum berries. If you want something a little more exotic, try bouvardia, oriental cymbidium orchids and sculptural arum lilies. For a winter posy, spray roses and tiny lily alstroemeria make a glorious combination with jewel-hued anemones.

If you would like further information on flowers, their seasons, trends and arrangement ideas and you're online, you can access information from the Flowers and Plants Association on their Web site: www.flowers.org.uk.

Flower Power

Seasonal Flowers

It's a nice touch to use some seasonal flowers in your arrangements; the following guide shows you the availability of flowers by season:

- **Spring** – wax flower, lily of the valley, sweet william, broom, hyacinth, African corn lily, grape hyacinth, daffodil, cherry blossom, turban buttercup, lilac, snowball tree;

- **Summer flowers** – monkshood, Nile lily, lady's mantle, ornamental onion, bellflower, marguerite, sweet william, foxtail lily, clarkia, sunflower, peony, poppy, tuberose, bluebell, goldenrod, throatwort, Queen Fabiola lily;

- **Autumn** – love lies bleeding, belladonna lily, Chinese aster, cockscomb, montbretia, globe amaranth, sunflower, St John's wort, red hot poker, obedience plant, soapwort, scabious, stonecrop, goldenrod;

- **Winter** – wax flower, spurge, hyacinth, daffodil, sugarbrush, lilac.

Flowers Available All Year Round

Ginger lily, Peruvian lily, Queen Anne's lace, pineapple, dill, painters' palette, snapdragon, butterfly weed, September flower, bottlebrush, orchid, Singapore orchid, carnation, snow-on-the-mountain, prairie gentian, Barbeton daisy, flame lily, baby's breath, lobster claw, safari sunset, lily, statice, loosestrife, stock, bells of Ireland, Jersey lily, dancing orchid, chincherinchee, moth orchid, rose, goldenrod, bird of paradise, speedwell, arum lily.

Flowers Available Most Seasons

Mimosa, yarrow, floss flower, kangaroo paw, Michaelmas daisy, orach, drumstick flower, amaryllis, sweet pea, slipper orchid, tulip.

Fake Flowers

Some may prefer silk or plastic flowers to decorate the wedding and reception venues. Silk flowers may also be used for the bride's and attendants' bouquets and for the headdress(es). These can be as effective as fresh flowers, the only disadvantage being that they have no scent. The advantages are that there is no danger of wilting and they will last long after your wedding as a memento of your special day.

The Language of Flowers

Think of the Shakespearian quote, '... there's Rosemary, that's for Remembrance'. Flowers have long held a significance beyond their simple beauty. In Britain, floral language became popular in Victorian times as a method of communication for lovers. Each flower carried its own personal code. It can be fun for a wedding to tap into this Victorian language of love and to choose flowers that represent your sentiments for each other. So, if you want to know your begonias from your bluebells, check out the following list for the final word in plant and flower speak:

Amaryllis	splendid beauty, pride
Arum lily	magnificent beauty
Azalea	temperance
Bluebell	constancy, forgive and forget
Cactus	warmth
Camelia	unpretending excellence

Campanula	White – gratitude
Carnation	Pink – woman's love
	Red – 'alas for my poor heart'
	Striped – refusal (to avoid)
	Yellow – disdain (to avoid)
Celosia	affection, individuality
Chrysanthemum	Red – 'I Love You'
	White – truth
	Yellow – slighted love (to avoid)
Cyclamen	diffidence
Daffodil	regard, chivalry
Dahlia	good taste
Fern	sincerity
Forget-me-not	true love, 'the key to my heart'
Freesia	friendship
Garden pink	pure love
Geranium	graceful, bewitching smile
Gladiolus	strength of character
Hibiscus	delicate beauty
Hyacinth	Blue – constancy
	White – unobtrusive loveliness
Iris	Yellow – flame of love
Ivy	friendship, fidelity in marriage
Jasmine	White – amiable
	Yellow – grace, elegance
Larkspur	lightness
Lilac	Purple – first emotions of love
	White – youthful innocence
Easter Lily	sweet-natured
Lily of the valley	return of happiness
Longi (longiflorum) Lily	pure and modest
Love lies bleeding	hopeless, not heartless
Mimosa	sensitivity, secret love
Narcissus	self-esteem, female ambition

Orange Blossom	bridal festivities, virginity, 'your purity equals your loveliness'
Orchid	longevity, elegance
Palm	victory
Peony	bashfulness
Pineapple	'you are perfect'
Ranunculus	'you are rich in attractions'
Rose	love and good fortune
	Crown of blooms – reward of virtue
	Large bright pink – meet me by moonlight
	Red – eternal love
	Red and White together – unity
	Rosebuds – pure and lovely
	Single stem – simplicity
	Small Yellow – 'thou art all that is lovely'
	White – truth
	White with pink blush – only for thee
Rudbeckia	justice
Snowdrop	hope
Solidago	encouragement
Star of Bethlehem	purity
Stock	lasting beauty
Sunflower, dwarf	adulation
Sweet pea	departure, delicate pleasures
Tulip	Red – declaration of love
	Striped – beautiful eyes
Veronica	fidelity
Violet	faithfulness, modesty
Zinnia	thoughts of absent friends

Stress Busters

▌ Choose a florist well in advance.

▌ For the wedding party, consider the bride's bouquet and possibly headdress, bridesmaids' bouquets, mothers' corsages and the groom's, fathers', best man's and ushers' buttonholes.

▌ In a church, consider decorating the altar, pulpit, lectern, windowsills, font, columns, church entrance, chancel steps and pew ends.

▌ Try to find a local florist to cut costs.

▌ Bring along some fabrics and even sketches to give an idea of the bride's and attendants' clothes.

▌ Bring along some photographs of the interior of the wedding and reception venue.

▌ Think of seasonal flowers.

▌ Think not only of the appearance but also of the scent of the flowers.

19 *Photographs and Videos*

The average amount spent on wedding photography is £389 and on video £297. A record of your wedding will be with you for the rest of your life so make sure you choose your photographer carefully. Start by asking family and friends for recommendations.

If you draw a blank, the Guild of Wedding Photographers and the Master Photographers' Association are both reputable organizations that require a professional standard of photography from their members. Both will send you a list of qualified members in your area, and are extremely helpful.

The Guild of Wedding Photographers can be contacted on 0161 928 3716. The Master Photographers' Association can be contacted on 01325 356 555.

Choosing Your Photographer

Alternatively, look a number up in the Yellow Pages. In either case, visit the shop or studio of a potential photographer and interview him or her thoroughly.

Ask to see some specimen albums. If you don't like what you see, find a different photographer. It is a case of personal preference, although there are some guidelines of things to look for.

Firstly, check that the album shows a good sample of one wedding and not the 'best ones' from a variety of occasions. Ask when the photographs were taken, and if everyone is wearing 1970s flares or 1980s clothes, don't touch the photographer with a barge pole, because he or she hasn't had a job for years.

Ask yourself, is there an interesting spectrum of shots? There should be a good mix of portrait and group shots. Do you have a good impression of the whole wedding from the album? If you're looking for photographs that capture the less formal side of the wedding, make sure the photographer is capable of taking animated and natural shots as well as formal ones.

A well-taken photograph should focus your eye on some part of the wedding festivities. Ask yourself whether your eye is distracted by irrelevant detail or whether the photographer has successfully focused attention on his or her intended subject. Also, think about clarity. Can you see the expressions on people's faces clearly?

If you're happy with the albums, the next stage is to ensure that what you see is what you get. Firstly, make sure the photographer you are interviewing is the one who is being booked for your wedding day. If it turns out to be someone else, ask to see samples of your photographer's work. If they can't do this for you, forget it and find another photographer.

Ask to see qualifications and evidence of being part of a professional association. Find out how much time the photographer thinks will be needed to do a good job. This is important, as you need to consider costs and the amount of intrusion on your day.

Check that the photographer is covered by his or her own insurance. In case of disaster this will cover the costs of any retakes.

Trust your gut instincts. The photographer will have a big part to play in your day. If he or she annoys you, don't make a booking, as you'll find the photographer even more irritating when he or she is telling you what to do. Discuss carefully the type of photographs you want. If the photographer seems inflexible or unsympathetic to your wishes, look elsewhere.

Cost and Type of Photographs

The price depends on the package and photographer. It is difficult to put a price on it, but a basic package could be anywhere upwards of £150. The best advice is to shop around.

Have interviews with as many photographers as possible so you can gauge what a reasonable estimate is for your wedding package. When you are quoted an overall price, check that development of prints, VAT and the photographer's travel costs are all included.

When deciding on the best deal for you, consider the following factors. Prices will depend on:

▌ the experience of the photographer and a successful track record;

▌ the amount of time the photographer spends at your wedding;

▌ the approximate number of photographs to be taken;

▌ the number of final pictures in your package;

▌ the quality of the album.

The Type of Photographs

It's up to you what you choose to take pictures of; the number of professional shots you arrange will depend on your budget. Traditional wedding pictures can include some of the following shots:

▌ **Arriving at the wedding ceremony:**

– Groom full length and close up

– Groom with best man – full length and close up

- Groom, best man and ushers

- Groom and father

- Groom and parents

Arrival of bridal party:

- Bridesmaids, pageboy/flowergirl

- Bridesmaids individually

- Bridesmaids and bride's mother

- Bride's mother

- Bride at carriage

- Bride and father

- Bride full length and close up

- Bride and bridesmaids

- Bride and bridesmaids and father

- Bride and parents

- Bride's father and vicar

- Bride and guests (grandmother or other important family)

- Family members

- Interior of church if permission given

▌ **During the ceremony:** Photography during the ceremony is sometimes not permitted, so check with your minister or registrar.

▌ **Signing the register:**

– Bride and groom signing the register

– Bride and groom and vicar receiving certificate

– Bride and groom and witnesses

– Bride and groom and parents

▌ **Bridal recession:**

– Couple at altar

– Bride and groom walking down the aisle

▌ **Outside:**

– Bride and groom at church door full length and close up

– Bride and groom and best man

– Bride and groom, best man and bridesmaids

– Bride and groom, best man and ushers

▌ **Families:**

– Bride and groom and bride's parents

– Bride and groom and groom's parents

Ideas for Extra Shots

Before the wedding: It is becoming customary for the photographer to visit the bride and her family and take some informal shots as they prepare for the wedding. It's also a nice idea if the photographer visits the groom, as you end up with a full account of the whole day.

Another option is to take photographs of guests as they arrive at the reception. Individual portraits of single guests and couples snapped as they enter the reception venue are a wonderful memento of your big day. This can be pricey. If this exceeds your photography budget, ask a friend to take the snaps for you.

Alternatively, buy some disposable cameras. Hand them out at the reception for guests to take a record of their evening. Ask guests to give them in at the end of the evening. Have them developed once for yourself and you'll have a fun and lively record of friends and family and even yourselves from every corner of your wedding festivities! It will probably be too expensive for you to develop a copy of these for your guests. However, you could make the negatives available for any guests who would like to make their own copies.

Black and White or Colour

Colour photographs are great for a vibrant record of what is after all a wonderful and exciting occasion. Black and white photographs can look romantic and timeless and sometimes make people look more attractive as blemishes are less likely to stand out. If you can afford it, you could order some of both, as then you have mementoes with the advantages of both styles of photograph.

DESI FONTAINE STUDIOS
p h o t o g r a p h y

Whether you are about to get married in a religious ceremony with a traditional reception, pledge thy troth while hanging upside down from a trapeze or if you simply plan to turn up together at a register office - just the two of you - to exchange vows, you will need to choose a professional photographer, who will be sensitive to catching the real spirit of the special day.

London based lady photographer, Desi Fontaine says, "When prospective clients come to see me I show them albums of complete weddings. It's very important that couples see a consistent flow of work throughout a wedding. I like them to tell me what they like about different styles of photography. The fashion at the moment seems to be for very natural looking photography, and lots of black and white shots, but the bride and groom have to be aware that these moments are rarely just spontaneous. Most often, a photographer has put 'input' and ideas into the shots to make it seem as if it has just happened naturally.

It is very important at this early stage that the bride and groom have a real sense of how long the photography will take. I don't want them to feel as if they've spent all of their reception in a photo shoot. The photography should blend in with the day and not take over. Couples now are having less and less group shots and more candid shots of guests, many couples are choosing 100-150 photographs for their album.

My own daughter is getting married this summer and I won't be putting any 'gimmicky' shots into the album. Today's gimmicks could be tomorrow's 'heads in champagne glass' type shots and I tend to stay well clear of those. I feel it's so important that the photographer and couple get on well together - then we can achieve terrific shots together.

Desi Fontaine can be contacted on 020 8878 4348 or Fax 020 8392 2514

What to Do if Disaster Strikes

If you've done your homework well before the wedding, you narrow down the chances of this happening. You should check that your photographer has insurance to cover the costs of retaking in case the pictures are spoiled or lost – it does happen. Your photographer's cover will pay for the photos to be retaken.

Of course, this will not be on your wedding day. If you have your own wedding insurance policy, check what you are entitled to. Some policies can offer up to £2,000 compensation for ruined photos. In the event that there is any disagreement with a photographer who is part of a professional association, the association will act as a mediator between photographer and client to try to clear up the mess.

Budget Tips

If you're low on funds you could ask a friend to take the photographs for you. Try and find one who is a talented photographer. Don't trust your wedding day memories to someone who is likely to stick his or her finger across the lens. It's usually best if you can afford a professional even for a few poses, so you're guaranteed to receive some cracking shots.

Video

Nowadays many people hire a video maker on their wedding day. For videos the same advice applies – shop around – as there are some real charlatans in this expanding industry as well as some professional filmmakers.

The Institute of Videography (IOV) is a good port of call for advice and recommendations. The IOV is a regulated body that awards membership to video makers of professional standard.

Although the average couple spends under £300 for a video, a professional job will probably cost you anywhere between £500 and £750. If your videographer costs under £300, it's probably because domestic rather than professional equipment is being used. Your photographer might also be able to offer a video service. Again, make sure you check that the video maker has professional indemnity insurance. Contact The Institute of Videography on 0345 413626.

Stress Busters

▌ If you don't know where to start, contact a professional organization like the Master Photographers' Association or the Guild of Wedding Photographers.

▌ Book well in advance, good wedding photographers are in demand.

▌ Meet any prospective photographers in person and ask to see samples of previous wedding work.

▌ Depending on what you are looking for, check the photographer can produce the type of formal and informal shots that you want.

▌ Don't choose someone who can't be flexible.

▌ Be clear about what you are looking for and decide on the exact package.

▌ Make sure the photographer you are interviewing is the one who is turning up on your wedding day.

▌ Check that hidden costs like developing and transport of equipment etc are included in your quote.

20 *Wedding Lists*

The History

The ancient tradition of buying gifts for the bride and groom goes back to the days when a 'dowry' was paid by the bride's father to his future son-in-law and family. The reason for this was that as the husband-to-be would have to keep his wife for the rest of her life he should be rewarded (or even bribed) at the start. If the bride's father were not wealthy enough to provide an adequate dowry, friends and family would help out by contributing either money or gifts. When the custom of paying a dowry died out, the practice of buying gifts continued as a way of helping the couple to set up home.

The concept of an actual 'wedding list' dates back to 1920 when the General Trading Company in London set up its first bridal gift service. Back then, lists of givers and gifts were published in the press, one stage on from the Show of Presents concept that Scots know and love. Up until 10 years ago the wedding list phenomenon was not widespread in this country but now it is seen as the norm.

What Is a Wedding List?

The point of a wedding list is to help newly married couples set up home together and provide them with a basis to start their married life. Couples who have been living together for some time, or who individually have property of their own, usually have most of the basic equipment they need, but are now turning to specialist wedding list companies for something more interesting and exciting.

You can put anything you like on your wedding list – pots, pans, towels, barbeques, books or subscriptions. It is entirely up to you what you ask for but remember, you may not get it!

The best time to compile a wedding list is no more than three months and no less than six weeks before the wedding. Some shops allow the list to remain open for another four to six weeks after the wedding for the benefit of the odd forgetful guest or anyone who hasn't quite found the time to buy a gift.

Should You or Shouldn't You?

It used to be that sending a wedding list with your invitation to the ceremony was looked on as bad form. Nowadays, though, the concept has become so popular with guests as well as the happy couple that it is quite acceptable to put a little note in with the invitation giving the name and address of the store holding your wedding list and their phone number.

Christine Prunty, editor of _Wedding and Home_ magazine, says, 'A lot of people are still embarrassed to admit to having a wedding list or they're worried about all the old-fashioned rules and traditions. But these days anything goes, so you can ask for classic crystal or even a wacky loo brush if that's what you want. Guests find wedding lists make their lives easier so there's no stigma about having one these days.'

Organizing Your Own Wedding List

Preparing your wedding list is a very important part of getting married. With so many crucial decisions to be made, it is essential to have choice, information and assistance available to you. Your wedding list can take one of two forms. The first is where you make up your own list and distribute it to those who ask to see it. When they have chosen a gift, it is returned with that item crossed off.

Since your invitations will have been posted 8–12 weeks before your wedding day, there will be plenty of time for your list to do the rounds. So that the correct items are chosen, you should include the manufacturer's name, model and colour. It is traditional that the bride-to-be's mother handles and circulates the wedding list.

You may like to do your own wedding list if you want all sorts of different gifts from different places and not just from the same shop, although there are now quite a few companies who, for a fee, will help you compile a list of items from various sources and administer it for you (see later in this chapter).

Companies/Shops that Offer a Wedding List Service

The second form your wedding list can take, which is preferred by most couples today, is where a particular shop or department store holds your wedding list. Most major stores provide a wedding list service where you make up your list after browsing through the store at your leisure. Also, as part of the service, a store will manage your wedding list so that when your guests telephone or visit the store, the item chosen is removed from your list. After your wedding, the store will send you a list of who has purchased what so you know who to send your thank-you letters to.

Stores that have many branches across the country, such as Debenhams, Argos and Marks & Spencer, offer further advantages. The greatest benefit is that they have a catalogue from which you can compile your wedding list – all from

Rowenta

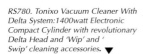

RS780. Tonixo Vacuum Cleaner With Delta System:1400watt Electronic Compact Cylinder with revolutionary Delta Head and 'Wip' and ' Swip' cleaning accessories. ▼

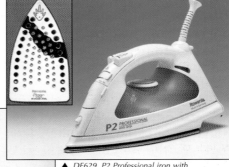

▲ *DE629. P2 Professional iron with Airglide precision soleplate.*

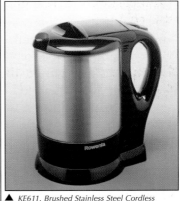

▲ *KE611. Brushed Stainless Steel Cordless Jug Kettle with Concealed Element*

Full Rowenta range includes floorcare, irons, kettles, coffee makers, kitchen essentials, dental care, fans and air conditioners.

Rowenta (UK) Ltd.
1a Langley Business Centre,
Station Road, Slough, Berkshire SL3 8PH
Tel: 0800 616413 for Stockists
Web Site: www.rowenta.co.uk
E-mail: rowenta@rowenta.co.uk

Visibly better!

GERMANY

the comfort of your own home, thus saving many hours of browsing around a store. Once you have made your selection, they will produce as many lists as you need so you can send a copy to anyone who asks.

Your guests can then buy your chosen gifts from the store most local to them, and since the stores are computer linked, your wedding list is updated as each purchase is made.

Many stores now also have Internet access, which means that once you have compiled your list they will post it on the Internet and your guests can access it themselves (using a password), which is even easier than visiting the shop or buying something over the telephone.

Using the wedding gift services of single product companies such as Royal Doulton, Wedgewood and Edinburgh Glass is becoming increasingly popular, especially with couples who already have most items needed for their home. By choosing a company such as this, a couple has the opportunity to acquire something of quality that will last for a considerable number of years and can be added to long after their wedding to make their collection complete.

Whatever type of wedding list you decide on, it's important that you include a wide range of items to cater for all budgets.

You may also wish to put some more expensive items on your list so that some of your family and friends can pool their resources to buy you something really special. Your list should also have more gifts on it than you expect to receive so that the last person to see the list still has a wide range of items to choose from.

Christine Prunty says you should have a wide range of gifts on the list. 'Wedding gifts are meant to last a long time,' she says, 'so make sure you have some china or glass that you will use for years. But you should also have small cheap items like towels and salt cellars. I think it's fun to have a few purely indulgent items on too that you would never buy yourself, like a Phillip Starck loo-brush!'

Here are some examples of the wedding list services on offer:

Debenhams
1 Welbeck Street
London W1M 7PA
Tel: 0171 408 4444

The Service:	Debenhams has a special wedding adviser in each of its stores around the country. Also available is an electronic scanner that you can take round the store with you, rather than having to write down code numbers, but you need to book in advance for this service. Guests can purchase gifts either in person at their nearest store or by telephoning any Debenhams shop with a wedding service. If guests decide to telephone their order, they should be wary as telephone lines are extremely busy during the peak months between May and August. There is also an optional gift-wrapping service but at an extra cost of £3.50 per gift paid for by the guests. Unfortunately this does not include large bulky presents.
Price:	No charge
Special Offers:	Debenhams will give each couple the equivalent in gift vouchers or 5 per cent of the total purchase.
Delivery:	A charge of £3.50 is levied on all gifts delivered in the UK but obviously not on any gifts purchased and taken out of the store. In peak times Debenhams need at least three weeks notice to

arrange convenient times for delivery of gifts.

Internet Service: Yes. Web site is www.debenhams.co.uk

John Lewis
Oxford Street
London W1A 1EX
Tel: 0171 499 1977

(or) Holmes Farm Way
Cressex Centre
High Wycombe HP12 4NW
Tel: (01494-443 681)

(or) Peter Jones
Sloane Square
London SW1W 8EL
Tel: 0171 730 0200

The Service: Three of the John Lewis Partnership's 23 department stores operate a computerized Bride's Book service for wedding present lists. All the prospective bride and groom need to do is to register with the Brides department and then go round the shop compiling a list of items they would like to select as gifts. Details are then entered into the computer and can be changed and added to whenever necessary.

At any given time John Lewis in Oxford Street and Peter Jones in Sloane Square can have up to 1,600 'live' lists. One of the reasons why these shops are quite popular with future brides is that they offer a large range of merchandise to choose from.

The downside is that John Lewis has no central buying or selling system, so your friends and relations have to buy from the exact store where you set up your list. They also don't have an Internet service so it is not very convenient. Basically your guests need to telephone, or come into the branch in person and select whatever gift appeals to them from the couple's list. These are then marked off and despatched to the bride, either at regular intervals or in one large delivery after the wedding.

Price: No charge

Special Offers: None

Delivery: Free of charge within a 30-mile radius. If over 30 miles, the couple have a choice of either agreeing to pay £25.00 for the whole bulk of presents to be delivered at once or a £3.00 levy is charged on individual items bought by family and friends.

Internet Service: No

Harrods
Knightsbridge
London SW1X 7XL
Tel: 0171 730 1234

The Service: Each couple registering with Harrods Wedding Department is provided with a Bridal Work Book which contains detailed information on the availability of glass, silver, linen, kitchenware, etc. Couples then browse round the departments in question, and introduce themselves to a member of staff whose job it is to show them the gifts chosen and tick them off in their book.

Back in the bridal department, the book containing all the requests is transferred onto a computer and a personal Bridal Administrator is then appointed to handle the Bridal Work Book on the couple's behalf. Guests can request a copy at any time, which can be either sent or faxed. Once guests have decided on what they want to buy, they can either come into Harrods and personally view the gift or telephone their choice direct to the couple's personal administrator.

Every two to three weeks, the personal administrator sends letters and updates to the bride of what has been purchased. Any gifts that are not wanted Harrods allow to be exchanged for alternative items of the same value.

Price: No charge

Special Offers: Credit is given of 3 per cent of the total value of items purchased. This means, for example, that if £4,000-worth of gifts are sold, the bride and bridegroom are given a credit of £120 to spend at Harrods at any time.

Delivery: Delivery is free in mainland UK. Overseas is charged according to destination but this can be claimed back by way of VAT.

Internet Service: Yes. Web site is www.harrods.co.uk

Liberty
Regent Street
London WlR 6AH
Tel: 0171 734 1234

The Service: Liberty was founded over 100 years ago and originally dedicated to finding unusual and sometimes ethnic merchandise from all over the world, and it's this principle that is still adhered to today. Couples need to register in person at least 6 to 12 weeks before the date of their wedding. Once registered, Liberty supplies you with 'guests' cards' that should be enclosed with your wedding invitation. The card simply informs guests that your wedding list is at Liberty and briefly explains how the service operates. Once you have decided on your list, a team of experienced wedding list consultants will be on hand to assist guests in selecting an appropriate gift.

If guests are unable to come personally to the store, on request a list can be either faxed or sent to them. Gifts can be ordered over the telephone and all major credit cards are accepted.

Price: Free
Special Offers: None
Delivery: Delivery is free to anywhere within mainland UK. Gifts are delivered in bulk after the wedding but this could amount to two deliveries.Couples are asked to advise Liberty of the most convenient time to arrange delivery, principally after they return from their honeymoon.
Internet Service: No

Argos Wedding List Service Department
489–499 Avebury Boulevard
Central Milton Keynes MK 2NW
Tel: 01908 600557 or 0870 600 2525

The Service: The most convenient and appealing aspect of Argos's Wedding List Service Department is that brides and grooms can all but plan their wedding list from their front room. All you need do is phone for an Argos catalogue, which is full of all sorts of things you would need to set up home together. Simply select the items you decide for your wedding list and then speak to the Wedding List Service Department who will process the list into their computer. Guests can then purchase wedding gifts with the minimum of fuss.

The computer instantly records what has been purchased and ensures that no item is bought twice. Argos suggests you allow at least three months prior to the date of your wedding to prepare your wedding list.

Copies of wedding lists are supplied free to guests. All guests need to do when purchasing a gift is go to any Argos store and ask for the couple's list by name, choose a gift and tell the assistant at the till which gift has been selected. This is then recorded in the computer and, after payment, delivered to the till ready for you to take away.

Price: No charge
Special Offers: None

Delivery: None
Internet Service: Yes. Web site is www.argos.co.uk

Habitat
Tottenham Court Road
London W1P 9LD
Tel: 0171 351 1211

The Service: Couples can go to any Habitat branch and compile their own wedding list. Gifts can be selected either from a simple guide sheet provided by consultants working in the Bridal Department or by visiting individual departments and personally selecting wedding gifts. Once the list is complete, it is transferred onto a computer and this then enables guests to select gifts without having to turn up in person.

Free copies of the wedding list can be faxed or sent to guests on request. Habitat says that at least 50 per cent of all gifts are purchased over the telephone. The department sends out regular updates of who has purchased what. Habitat is also flexible about exchanging unwanted gifts. The list is kept open for up to two weeks after the wedding day for late buyers, which is handy for busy guests or those from abroad who can't get through in time.

Price: No charge
Special Offers: None
Delivery: A charge of £3 is levied on all gifts but this includes wrapping. All gifts are delivered in one lot two weeks after the wedding.

Internet Service: Yes. Web site is www.habitat.co.uk but they do not post your wedding list on the Internet.

The Wedding List Company
91 Walton Street
London SW3 2HP
Tel: 0171 584 1222

The Service: The Wedding List Company offers an exclusive personal and individual service to bride and groom as well as guests. All you have to do is make an appointment with one of The Wedding List's consultants and discuss with them the sort of gifts you are looking for to set up home. They will be more than happy to give you all the help and advice you need, and even advise you on how to construct your wedding list, particularly if there are a number of priority presents such as a large dinner service that may need to be split up and purchased by several guests.

The Wedding List Company also exclusively handles lists for top Mayfair china and homeware shop Thomas Goode. The company will supply gift cards, but you can have your own personal card attached to the gift.

Price: No charge
Special Offers: None
Delivery: Depending on availability, first delivery takes approximately three weeks from the date the final list is agreed. Note that

glass and china can take up to 4 to 12 weeks, especially if they have been ordered from abroad. Delivery to London postal districts is free, but outside London a minimal charge is levied.

Internet Service: No

The Gift List Company
37 Blandford Street
London W1H 3AE
Tel: 0171 935 3100

The Service: For a fee of £75.00, The Gift List Company has a number of personal shopping consultants who will spend a day with you, escorting you around London's most prestigious shops. You can either choose gifts from your shopping day or relax over a cup of coffee or a glass of wine and select your list from The Gift List's exclusive premises in Blandford Street.

Price: £75.00 if you use the personal shopping consultant service.

Special Offers: After the wedding, you are entitled to 10 per cent discount on any items purchased from The Gift List Company.

Delivery: Delivery is free within the M25. Quotations are available for delivery outside this area. Also, should you require your gifts to be stored, this is free up to three months but charged at £30.00 a week thereafter.

Internet Service: Yes. Web site is www.thegiftlist.co.uk

The General Trading Company
Sloane Street
London SW1X 9BL
Tel: 0171 730 0411
(Wedding Services Manager Annette Thomas, ext 219)

The Service:	The General Trading Company is one of the oldest established wedding list providers. GTC was founded in 1920 and to this day remains a family business, which prides itself on offering quality, stylish and individual merchandise. It is the one shop that is willing to keep your wedding list open for up to two years after you have married. Why? Well, GTC feels that by offering this service, it will encourage family and friends to look for special gifts for future occasions as well as proving helpful for your personal reference. To arrange to have your wedding list at GTC, all you have to do is arrange for an appointment with one of GTC's experienced consultants, who will escort you round the store and help you organize your wedding list.
Price:	No charge
Special Offers:	None
Delivery:	Free delivery in central London and they will quote a price for out-of-town addresses.
Internet Service:	No

The Present Connection
22 Battersea Rise
London SW11 1EE
Tel: 0171 228 4002

The Service:
The Present Connection offers an interesting but somewhat unusual wedding list service operated entirely through the Internet. At the time of going to print their Web site was still under construction, but why not check it out at www.present.co.uk. Couples can choose from two styles of wedding list, either the traditional present list, where items selected are ordered and delivered immediately, or the credit list, which offers greater flexibility when selecting gifts.

The service includes: Initial consultation to discuss your wedding list requirements, compilation of the list, interior design advice and guidance, notification cards, administration of your wedding list including regular updates, thank-you cards, your list on their Web site, and delivery of your wedding presents in central London.

Price:
The Present Company charges £60 for preparing your list but you are guaranteed a repayment fee providing that the purchase value of your listed wedding gifts exceeds £2,000.00. Every £25.00 spent on your list equals 1 point. 1 point = £1.00.

Special Offers: None

Delivery: Deliveries are free of charge within Greater London and can be arranged at any time between 10.00 am and 8.00 pm. All deliveries outside greater London will be charged at cost.

Internet Service: Yes. Web site is www.present.co.uk

Marks & Spencer Wedding Bureau
Freepost
PO Box 288
Warrington WA1 2BR
Tel: 01925 858502

The Service: Marks & Spencer's Wedding Bureau is managed by a team of experienced staff available to help and assist you in selecting your gifts from the products listed in their Wedding List catalogue. This can be done in relative comfort at home and, after you have selected what you require, all you then have to do is return the completed forms to Marks & Spencer. At the top of your list you can compile an appropriate message for your guests, either thanking them for looking at your list or highlighting a number of items you would most like to receive. You will also be given a password; this prevents anyone from making amendments to your list without your prior consent. Each month Marks & Spencer sends a wedding list update informing you what gifts have been purchased and the availability of the remaining gifts.

Price: No charge

Special Offers: None

Delivery:	Delivery is available to anywhere in the UK including Northern Island, but they do not deliver to the Republic of Ireland or the Channel Islands. First arrange a convenient day for delivery, as it is not always guaranteed that they can deliver when you particularly want them to. They will keep the gifts free of charge for up to six months, should that be necessary.
Internet Service:	No

The Wedding List Services Limited
127 Queenstown Road
Battersea
London SW8 3RH
Tel: 0171 978 1118

Service:	The Wedding List Services is another company offering Internet access. For those busy couples who don't have time to browse round shops choosing their wedding list, this is an ideal way of getting a list together with the minimal of fuss and bother. Choices can be made from the Wedding List Services' own database, available via the Internet, of over 40,000 items. Although the images are not scanned, this is a far easier way of choosing gifts if you know what you want.

The main way people choose is by coming into the office and looking at samples and pictures of items and gaining valuable advice from staff members.

Price:	£35 if the list is on the Internet, otherwise no charge.
Special Offers:	Close family relations can have 10 per cent discount on purchases over £500 in the cutlery, crystal or china departments.
Delivery:	Free in the London area but out of town they charge a normal courier fee.
Internet Service:	Yes. Web site is www.wedding.co.uk

On the Day

It is up to you whether you want the gifts delivered before or during the day of the wedding. Some people like to have the gifts on display but if you are going away on honeymoon immediately and are worried about leaving them behind, make sure you arrange with the wedding list providers exactly where and when you want the items delivered. Make sure you get the place and time agreed in writing. This way, if the gifts are delivered to the wrong place or at the wrong time you will be able to complain to the company and, probably, get some compensation.

Many of the stores mentioned are nationwide. Below are regional stores that have wedding list services; the addresses and contact numbers can be added to or replace the London ones:

Debenhams
1–5 St James
Barton
Bristol
Avon BS99 7JX
Tel: 0117 929 1021

John Lewis
Wilmslow Road
Cheadle
Cheshire SK8 3BZ
Tel: 0161 491 4422

Marks & Spencer
42 High Street
Birmingham B4 7SS
Tel: 0121 643 4511

Thank-you Notes

After you receive a gift or have been notified that one has been chosen from your list, you must send a personal and handwritten thank-you letter. Pre-printed thank-you cards are not considered suitable and should be avoided. Although it may seem easier to sit down and write all your thank-you letters when you return from your honeymoon, you will find it a much less daunting task to write them as you receive your gifts.

If you have been sent any cheques or gift vouchers, your thank-you letter should say what you propose buying with them. This will give the donor much comfort in knowing that they have contributed to something you need in your home. When you sign your thank-you letter, the woman's name is always written before the man's, eg Yours, Sarah and Michael Smith.

Insuring Your Gifts

You will probably be surprised by the total value of all the wedding gifts you may receive. It would be sensible to check your home contents insurance policy to ensure that you have sufficient cover if they are damaged or stolen. However, you may find that although your gifts are covered if they are kept in your own home, they may not be covered if they are damaged or stolen while they are somewhere else, such as your reception venue or another family member's home. For peace of mind you should make sure your wedding gifts are insured against accident, loss, theft or damage outside your home.

A number of companies offer special wedding insurance and they all include insuring the gifts. WeddingSure from D J Hine & Co (0161 438 0000) has different levels of cover for various incidents from loss of the wedding presents to cancellation of the whole thing. Ecclesiastical Direct offers similar packages (0800 336622) which will also insure you against the transport not turning up or the marquee not functioning properly. Methodist Insurance plc (0161 833 9696) has two basic packages covering the usual things.

Taking Gifts Back

It's quite possible that at least one of your wedding presents could go wrong. If you have had everything from the one shop it should be quite easy to take something back as they will have a record of the purchase.

But generally, the most important thing to remember if you are not happy with an item is that if you want to take something back to the shop, you must have some proof of purchase such as a receipt or a credit card statement. Without that you are unlikely to get satisfaction. How do you tactfully get the receipt from your aged auntie? It is easier to return an unwanted gift without the receipt to the store that held your wedding list.

Apart from that one simple rule, the game is not entirely clear. Very much depends on the attitude or mood of the shop manager. Take heart, though. The retail industry is under such pressure at the moment that many companies, large and small, are bending over backwards to keep your custom and may exchange goods or give you money back just to keep you friendly.

Legally, you are only entitled to a refund of any item if it was defective when you (or the giver) bought it. So if your lovely new designer juicer wouldn't even switch on when you got back from honeymoon, you are perfectly entitled to your money back or an exchange, so long as you have the receipt. If the juicer is in perfect condition, though, and you just don't like the colour, you have no legal right to an exchange or refund.

In most shops you must return all faulty goods within a 'reasonable' period, but the question of what is a reasonable time is open to dispute. Obviously it is not your fault if you take back a wedding present that was bought months in advance or if it was bought at a shop that is very difficult for you to get to. Here, again, you might like to remind the shop manager of how hard it is to keep customer loyalty these days and suggest that your custom is more important than this single sale.

However, most large shops operate 'goodwill policies' which means they will let you take back a present if you just don't like it. Some of them will only offer a credit note, and frankly you would do well just to take it. Marks & Spencer is famous for exchanging anything so long as it is in resaleable condition and they will often allow you to take it back a few months after it was bought.

Top Tips for Compiling a Perfect Wedding List

Judith Clare who runs the Debenhams wedding list service has these tips for brides-to-be:

- The secret to making the right choice is to trust your own style. Think about the life you're going to lead, stick to your own taste and don't be influenced by other people. If you want to put minimalist modern plates on an ornate dinner table, go right ahead.

▌ Combining different patterns means you get two looks for the price of one. Then you can arrange formal place settings with items from two complementary ranges.

▌ When choosing glassware, you need to think about your lifestyle before you make a decision. Thinking about this will give you a better idea of what kind of dinner service and glassware you want and how many items to register.

▌ When you're choosing fine crystal, hold it up to the light. It should be perfectly clear with no blemishes and make a noise like a bell when you lightly tap it. If you're not sure what kind of pattern you want, look at your dinner service and pick a patterned glass that complements it for instant harmony, and then register for the same number of glassware sets as dinner plates you have ordered.

▌ Make a few notes before you start shopping to cut out confusion when you see the range on offer.

▌ A basic set of casual china should include one dinner plate, side plate, bowl, mug, teacup and saucer. You'll need a good tea set too and coffee mugs if you're a cappuccino fan.

▌ All good quality china tableware is marked underneath with a stamp and care instructions.

▌ Stainless steel cutlery is sold in different grades – less expensive brands are usually 13 per cent chrome while higher-quality ranges are around 18 per cent chrome and 10 per cent nickel.

Renowned saucepans and oven dishes, such as Le Creuset, are an investment that will last for decades. Knives are another piece of key equipment for the kitchen and you should register for at least one high-quality set with a knife block to make safe storage easier.

When you are choosing saucepans, look for a solid, heavy base and high sides to make adding and stirring liquids simple. And if you like to cook in a jiffy, non-stick pans are essential.

For the bathroom you will need at least six to eight towels or bath sheets, four to six hand towels, some face cloths and two bath mats.

Even if you've already got bedware, a fine set of bed linen is one of the basic luxuries you can permit yourself on your wedding list. Consider your colour scheme and the way you like to sleep (duvet? sheets and blankets? cotton or a cotton mix?) before you choose the bed linen you want.

Silver photo frames or photo albums are a great wedding list present as you can keep photos of your big day in them.

Top Wedding Gifts in the UK (according to John Lewis Partnership)

1   China

2   Glass

3   Kitchenware

4 Bed linen

5 Bath linen

6 Electrical

7 Silverware

8 Table accessories

9 Garden furniture

10 Lighting

21 *Honeymoons*

The honeymoon is a joyous relief after all the hard work of the lead-up to the wedding. It is a time to relax, spend some time alone – at last – and celebrate your new marriage. However, with the average UK couple spending about £2,446 on their honeymoon, this part of your marriage celebrations can be costly. But don't worry, you can do it in style without breaking the bank.

The First Night

To avoid spending your first night of wedded bliss on a cramped aeroplane or worse stuck in the airport, spend it somewhere near the reception venue. This could be a hotel, a quiet B&B, a friend's house or even your own. If you choose to pay for a room for the night, go and see it first to make sure it fits the bill.

If you cannot afford to splash out and are spending the night at home, think of ways to decorate your bedroom to make it feel exotic and romantic. First, tidy up and hide any eyesores – old socks and piles of magazines do not a romantic first night make.

Cover the room with flowers, drape material over familiar wardrobes, tables and any piles of junk. Change the lighting in your room. It makes a huge difference. Add some do-it-yourself low lighting by placing lamps and candles around the room and switch off any top lights. For an added touch of romance, have champagne waiting on ice.

Your Honeymoon

Tradition dictates that the groom chooses, books and pays for the honeymoon. Nowadays many couples make the decision together and share the financial burden.

More couples than ever before are spending their honeymoon in Britain according to a recent survey from *Wedding and Home* magazine. If you cannot afford a week away, spend a fabulous romantic break in a luxurious long weekend in a country hotel.

Call up the local tourist board of an area that you particularly love and ask for recommendations for a honeymoon venue. Alternatively, ask friends for ideas. If you have time, pop in to the hotel before you book to make sure everything is up to scratch.

For many couples a honeymoon has to include a little bit of tropical paradise. For those in search of coconut trees, azure seas and Pacific hideaways, you'll have to spend a little more. There is a vast range of luxurious packages to choose from, it's really a question of comparing quality and prices. Send away for brochures from reputable companies and ask friends for recommendations.

About 10 per cent of people now make their holiday bookings through teletext, so have a look there for inspiration. Whatever you do, don't book with a little-known company that you know nothing about. No matter how cheap the company is, it's not worth risking any disasters on your honeymoon.

Paying on Credit

Those whose bank accounts have been cleaned out by the wedding might want to borrow the money to pay for the honeymoon. If you are thinking about an overdraft, find out what rate of interest your bank will charge and then work out if it's the cheapest possible way to borrow. You might

find it more economical to borrow on your credit card. If you do decide to increase your overdraft, arrange it with the bank first. Charges for unauthorized borrowing are astronomical.

If you are paying off a holiday over a long term it is worth checking that your credit card has a competitive APR (annual percentage rate). If not, it's worth switching cards to one with a lower APR as you can make substantial savings.

Holidays are the third most popular reason for taking out personal loans. British Airways now offers loans from £500 up to £15,000 through their own financial service. Loans are currently offered at a competitive rate.

As with any loan, always shop around for the best deal. Do your maths. Find out if a deposit is required, work out what the total repayment will be and make sure you will be able to meet the monthly repayments. If there is an interest-free credit option always make sure you know if and when the free repayments will revert to interest repayments. Never sign a credit agreement of any sort until you have read it with a fine-tooth comb.

Holiday Currency

Credit cards and debit cards are useful to give you access to extra cash but they can carry heavy cash advance handling fees – around 1.5 per cent – and sometimes use poor rates of exchange. Cash machines are handy if you're in a major city but will often carry a minimum fee for each transaction and may not always be available. The best option is to take a mixture of travellers' cheques, foreign currency and a credit card or debit card for emergencies.

American Express gives the following advice on buying foreign currency:

▌ Don't wait to purchase your money abroad. High Street rates on the continent can result in a 10% loss of your holiday money.

▌ Exchange rates vary widely so compare rates carefully. Don't assume a low commission rate means a competitive exchange rate.

▌ Combine the commission rate and the exchange rate to find out the real cost of changing money.

▌ Flat commission rates are more likely to give you the best overall rate if you're changing a large sum.

▌ Find out if the bureau de change offers a commission-free buy-back policy. If it does, ask whether the offer is limited to large sums and if they charge a fee for the service.

Bermuda

fairytale weddings
& honeymoons

Beautiful blue skies, soft pink sands and turquoise seas.
An island paradise.

For the perfect start to married life call Bermuda Tourism on
0990 77 99 55
quoting reference DTG/W

▍ Check out the lesser known Dover Eurochange and TTT Moneycorp who are renowned for their good rates of exchange.

Passports

▍ Check passports are up to date.

▍ If the bride is changing her name she will need to have her passport changed in good time. To amend a passport you'll find the relevant passport form at any main post office. Leave yourself at least one month to ensure this is done in time and at least three months if you are applying between February and June.

▍ If the bride has not managed to arrange this in time, bring a copy of your marriage certificate along to the airport.

▍ Alternatively, travel under your maiden name. However, ensure your tickets are in your maiden name as well.

Bargain Hunting

▍ Many companies like Club Med offer discounts to newly weds, so shop around for the best deal. Club Med is offering a 25% discount for 1999.

▍ Fluctuating exchange rates mean that you will get more for your money in some countries than others. Go where your pound will stretch far.

▍ Book at the last minute and you are likely to make some sizeable savings. However, your choice will be incredibly limited. This is not a good idea if you have a fixed idea of where you want to go.

Star Treatment

▮ Wherever you go, make sure you let the hotel know you are honeymooners. You're likely to receive a complimentary bottle of champagne.

▮ Book a few surprises for your spouse, like a special car to take you to the hotel or breakfast in bed in the morning.

Planning

With so much to do planning your wedding, it's easy to overlook the final details of your honeymoon. Use our stress busters list to ensure nothing is overlooked.

Stress Busters

▮ Check passports are up to date.

▮ Have all inoculations at least two months in advance.

▮ Apply for a visa if needed at least one month before.

▮ If necessary get an international driving licence.

▮ Make sure you have travel insurance cover.

▮ Money/foreign currency.

▮ Always confirm tickets.

▮ Always confirm reservations.

22 *Wedding Insurance*

Despite the enormous cost of weddings, even though cover for weddings has been available for a decade and usually costs less than the bride's shoes, four out of five couples still do not protect their wedding day.

Anything and everything can go wrong on your wedding day. One couple were astonished to find that the reception venue they had booked months in advance burned down the night before they were due to marry. Another bride was astounded to find that her four-year-old brother had given her wedding dress a lick of red paint just a week before her wedding, while another unlucky pair were caught out when the caterer failed to turn up.

And it is not just personal disasters you have to worry about. One couple was sued when a waitress tripped over a photographer's tripod during the reception. The case cost £10,000 to settle.

The Cost of Insurance

Policies tend to cost between £40 and £50 for cancellation cover of between £3,000 and £6,000. The amount of cover you get for your money varies enormously, so be sure to shop around. Spend a morning on the telephone ringing round to find the best quote. It will be well worth it.

Wedding Insurance

In days of old a bride would rely on her father's dowry to ensure that her fiancé turned up at the appointed hour by the altar. A couple of burly brothers might also provide her with added security. However last minute disasters can still wreck the best-laid plans and newly designed wedding insurance policies have stepped in to provide peace of mind.

What could go wrong

Last month a certain groom, John, was indulging in the pre-matrimonial keep-fit regime when he tore his achilles tendon. Well, he may be a Greek demi-god to his intended but he is currently unable to walk and their wedding has had to be postponed for 3 months while he undergoes surgery and intensive physio-therapy. Sarah, his bride-to-be, is obviously less then happy about the situation but her father at least was relaxed about the whole affair. He had taken out insurance when he saw the bills mounting up.

Although there were a few tears following the horrific injury, Dad was able to promise his daughter the special wedding of her dreams, albeit delayed a short while, and all without any extra financial cost to the family. The insurance company paid all the deposits back to Sarah's father and also the remaining contracted balance to the suppliers who had not been able to find a replacement booking. They even paid for all the wedding invitations to be reprinted.

It is easy to find a horror story that has happened and there are plenty more which have meant that weddings have had to be postponed or cancelled at the last minute. Personal tragedies such as death or bereavement do unfortunately occur and reception venues burn down or go into liquidation with inconsiderate timing. That special dress does get damaged from time to time and photographers are human and can spoil a film or even forget to put one into the camera. Insurance is there for peace of mind, to protect those who cannot afford the financial consequences of an event outside of their control and to provide financial compensation where applicable.

Why take out cover

Almost all of us take out travel insurance when we go overseas on holiday. The majority also take extra comprehensive insurance on their motor cars and yet how many think of insuring their wedding? Surprisingly few. Only 1 in 5 couples insure one of the most expensive spending decisions in their life, their wedding. A wedding can be very stressful to organise and for a very small sum it is possible to have peace of mind that the event and accompanying clothes and accessories are protected.

Your legal position

If someone orders a service or agrees to purchase an item then they have actually entered into a legally binding contract with the supplier, even if it is only verbal. This means that if you cancel the contract, for whatever reason, you are liable for the consequences. So a deposit may be requested as a sign of good intent but your wedding caterer is legally entitled to request additional payment for the value of the services, which you would have taken if you had not cancelled.

When to take out cover

Wedding insurance covers a specific event in time and so the premium is the same whether you take cover the day before or a year in

What to Have Covered

Ensure that you have the following areas of cover:

▎ **Wedding outfits**

- Loss of or damage to all items of wedding clothing, including those of the bride, groom, bridesmaids, ushers and best man.

▎ **Photographs/Videos**

- Useful in the event that your photographs or video footage are spoiled or lost or the photographer doesn't advance. It therefore makes sense to take out cover as soon as possible, as you are then covered for a longer period of time. In reality most take out cover when they make their first financial commitment.

What are you covered for (and what not)

All policies vary in cover to some degree. However there are some specific exclusions which have to be included, such as the disinclination of the bride or groom to marry or known circumstances at the time of taking out a policy which are likely to give rise to a claim. The reason for this is that the policy holders should not profit from the cover that they take out. The insurance policy is there to assist in times of need and to compensate for unforseen disaster rather than to give newly-wed couples a financial kick-start to their marriage. The inclusion of such restrictions enables the insurance companies to keep the cost of the insurance low. However if you are aware of a particular circumstance, such as an ailing godfather, which worries you then all you need to do is let the insurance company know and they will normally agree to accept cover, often at no additional cost.

For example, CancelSure's policy is designed to cover all eventualities that are out of the bridal party's control which may result in cancellation of the wedding or loss and damage to expensive items such as the wedding dress, rings and wedding presents. The cover is best thought of as consisting of two major parts; one which covers you for the consequences of postponing or cancelling the wedding and the other which covers you for miscellaneous problems which may occur but will not force you to cancel the whole event. In addition most policies should cover you for any 3rd party liability that requires you to pay compensation to another party for accidental damage to them or their property. Finally it is often possible to take extra cover for the marquee which will pay out if there is accidental damage to it or the event is cancelled. Marquee cover is normally only available on the more expensive policies.

What does it cost

The premium is related to the amount of cover that you wish to take out. The lowest premium is around £50, which should cover approximately £3,000 of cancellation charges and around £500 to £1,000 of wedding dresses, presents and photographs. £150 premium would normally increase cancellation cover to £10,000 and give £2,000 cover for wedding dresses, presents etc. The higher premiums will also include cover against the marquee being damaged.

Summary

Stress is prevalent in every wedding and as the big day approaches, the pressure inevitably increases as the participants worry that something might go wrong. It is sensible therefore to protect yourself and purchase a little peace of mind for very little cost. No-one wants to make a claim but just knowing that you are covered will allow everyone to concentrate on enjoying the day.

0700 22 333 44
PO Box 22542, London, W8 7GB

turn up. Only necessary if your photographer doesn't have insurance.

▍ **Wedding gifts**

 – Covers the loss or damage of wedding gifts in the couple's possession, usually only for the day before the wedding and the wedding day.

▍ **Rings**

 – Loss of or damage to the rings. Usually up to seven days before the ceremony.

▍ **Damage to people and property**

 – Public liability cover of £1 million to £2 million against damage to people and property during the wedding; includes cover for the wedding cars.

What's Not Covered in Most Policies

▍ Marquees are sometimes excluded because they are prone to being blown down.

▍ Documentation problems when marrying abroad are also often excluded.

▍ Bad weather.

▍ Most policies do not cover for being jilted or for one spouse simply changing their mind. However, Cornhill Insurance offers the jilted up to £250 worth of stress counselling.

Top Five Wedding Day Disasters

▌ The bride's dress is ruined.

▌ Photographs do not come out.

▌ The bride or groom is too sick to attend.

▌ The caterer doesn't turn up.

▌ The wedding ring is lost.

23 *Second Time Around*

The numbers of remarriages have soared in recent years. By 1996 they accounted for around two-fifths of all marriages compared with a fifth in 1971. In 1996, both halves of nearly 54,000 couples who tied the knot in England and Wales had been married before. While for almost 65,000 couples, one partner had been married previously. The average age for remarriage is 38 for women and 41 for men.

Remarriage rates are twice as high for men as women. An astonishing 37.7 per cent of the male divorced and widowed population surveyed by the Office of National Statistics remarried in 1996.

Finding the perfect partner second time around can be a wonderful experience giving a second lease of life. However, even more so than at a first marriage, with the joining of clans come financial and legal issues to sort out.

Civil Requirements

Anyone marrying in Britain for the second time must have documentary evidence that the marriage has ended. This could be in the form of a death certificate or a decree absolute. It is important to make sure that your document is certified, as an uncertified document will not be accepted.

A certified copy is obtained from the court that decided your divorce – this can take about a week. If you are marrying overseas the decree absolute must be signed on the back by the district judges of the court.

"*..new romantics.*"

anello & *davide*
DIRECT

Changing Your Name

As with a first marriage, changing your name is not obligatory but is possible for either partner. Brides changing their names should make the same amendments to their official and personal documentation as outlined in the chapter on legal requirements for marriage.

Marrying Within a Faith

Certain religions allow people to remarry, including Islam, Judaism, the Society of Friends (Quakers) and Hinduism. Some, like Roman Catholicism, only allow a widow(er) to remarry. Even if partners cannot marry within their faith, as long as they have a civil divorce they will be able to marry second time around in a civil ceremony.

If you are a member of the Church of England and your former partner is still living, you could have problems trying to remarry in a religious ceremony. If you are single or widowed you have the right to be married within your parish church. However, if your divorced partner is still alive, the priest has the right to decide whether he or she will marry you. In the majority of cases divorcees are refused a second marriage in church because the promise made before God was to stay with your former partner for life. If you find this to be the case, ask for a service of prayer and thanksgiving after your civil ceremony. This is a good compromise that most ministers will gladly agree to.

Organize Your Finances

In terms of finance, marrying for a second time sometimes takes a bit more organizing. This is particularly relevant if you own a property. It is not very romantic, but sit down with a financial adviser before you marry and sort out how you will organize your joint money. For further advice, look at our chapter on organizing your married finances.

If you have children from a first marriage you might want to ensure that your assets are passed down to them rather than your husband or wife. If so, you will need to make a will as any former will is disregarded as soon as you marry. Do this through a solicitor.

A Civil Marriage

Couples marrying for the second time often feel more able to arrange a ceremony that suits them than they did at a first marriage. Mothers-in-law, fathers-in-law and extended family do not usually have such a big role the second time around. Most second marriages are civil. However, the wedding can be anything from a small ceremony with only two witnesses to a massive celebration. If either partner has grown-up children, it might be a nice gesture to ask your children to be witnesses to your marriage vows – but make sure they are happy about the forthcoming nuptials.

When Two Become One

Becoming a stepmother or stepfather can be both marvellous and challenging. Where children are concerned, the best advice is tread carefully and accept that they might not be as overjoyed about the marriage as you are. There are no hard or fast rules as to how to go about becoming a new family. You will largely have to play it by ear, but the main thing is to be understanding and patient. Do remember that you are the adults and do not resort to childish tactics because you feel hurt. It will only make things worse.

Once you decide to marry, the first decision you need to make is how to tell the children. It is up to each couple to decide when and how this is best done. Relate advises that you lower your expectations as to the reactions of your children. Remember that children, especially young children and adolescents, will probably be very much wrapped up in their own lives. So, do not necessarily read an adolescent sulk as being the result of your big news; it might be nothing to do with you. However, it is important that children have an outlet to help them adjust to the new situation. You should certainly inform the school of your changing circumstances and perhaps ask a favourite teacher or relative to speak to your child – they will probably feel happier speaking to another party about your marriage.

If you feel you could do with some extra help, contact your local Relate office. They also offer a counselling service for young people of secondary school age, called Relateen.

Stress Busters

- Check that all legal documentation is in place to show that your earlier marriage has ended.

- Organize your finances.

- Write a new will.

- If you are becoming a step-parent, be patient.

24 Organizing Your Married Finances

For one in five couples the main cause of discord in a relationship is money. When you wed it's important to think about the financial side of this romantic commitment. A joint account is practical, although you should be aware exactly what you are undertaking.

It is also a good idea to sort out what would happen to your money and assets if either of you died. Particularly so if you have children from a first marriage, as your children will end up with very little if you haven't made a will.

Should We Make a Prenuptial Contract?

In England and Wales prenuptial contracts have not really caught on, largely because they don't have a lot of weight in court. This is not the case in Scotland where the courts pay more attention to such contracts. An English judge will consider a prenuptial contract as one of many factors in a divorce settlement and may choose to totally disregard it depending on the circumstances at the time of divorce. At time of print, changes to the law are in the pipeline.

Should I Make a Will?

When you marry the last thing on your mind is death. But, taking time out to make a will is a simple way of avoiding legal costs in the event of either of you dying. If it's a second

TRADITIONAL ENGLISH HOMES

At Countryside we choose only the finest locations in which to build your new home, often representing the best 'new' address in the area. Every Countryside home is built with pride and meticulous attention to detail, combining the rich architectural heritage of a traditional English home with an interior layout that provides flexible living space and exceptional features and fittings to suit a modern lifestyle.

A new Countryside home will give you the tradition and style of a period or village home, with all the comfort, convenience and low maintenance of new.

KENT

Hunters Chase, Mascalls Court Road, Paddock Wood
3, 4 & 5 bedroom homes from £145,000 - £300,000
Stunning family homes in this picturesque yet convenient location in the Kentish countryside.
Telephone: 01892 837100

St. Mary's Island, Chatham
2, 3, & 4 bedroom homes from £85,000 - £250,000
A superb range of new homes to choose from, each with an outstanding specification throughout and everything you need for a modern lifestyle within this exciting island setting.
Telephone: 01634 890900

GLOUCESTERSHIRE

Wellington Place, Cheltenham
2 & 3 bedroom apartments from £149,950 to £300,000
Wellington Place will restore Priory Parade to its former Regency splendour, with the 32 magnificent apartments becoming one of the most prestigious addresses to have in Cheltenham.
Telephone: 01242 701178

SOMERSET

Fallowfield Village, Hallatrow
4 & 5 bedroom homes from circa £138,000
Fallowfield Village features carefully grouped family homes designed in the traditional Somerset vernacular. Each home has authentic architectural detailing and their successful layout has recently received a design award.
Telephone: 01761 453862

LANCASHIRE

The Nursery, Prescott Road, Ormskirk
4 & 5 bedroom detached homes from £210,000
A fine range of superb new homes with an outstanding specification set in an ideal location.
Telephone: John Ryder - 01695 575271

Loxwood, Walton le Dale, Preston
4 bedroom detached homes from £124,000
Highly individual new homes set in the leafy environment of Walton Park.
Telephone: Margaret Martin - 01772 335306

ESSEX

Beaulieu Park, Chelmsford
Prices from £163,000 - £435,000
Beaulieu Park, hailed by Henry VIII as a 'beautiful place', will certainly become 'the' address to have in Chelmsford, featuring an outstanding range of new Countryside homes, reflecting a rich architectural heritage.
Telephone: 01245 469657

HERTFORDSHIRE

The Village, Bishop's Stortford
Prices from £127,000 - £575,000
The Village in the traditional new community of St Michaels Mead, carefully re-creates the local vernacular of Hertfordshire's prettiest villages with a range of fine new 2, 3, 4 and 5 bedroom homes.
Telephone: 01279 834324

OTHER NEW HOMES ALSO AVAILABLE IN

ESSEX • HERTFORDSHIRE
Telephone: 01277 690660
KENT • SURREY • SUSSEX
Telephone: 01372 370130
BRISTOL • GLOUCESTERSHIRE • GWENT SOMERSET • MONMOUTHSHIRE
Telephone: 01454 202208
MERSEYSIDE • NORTH YORKSHIRE CHESHIRE • CLEVELAND
Telephone: 01925 248900

Show Homes open every day, 10.30am to 5.30pm
Prices correct as at 15.6.99

Countryside RESIDENTIAL

e-mail cpplc@aol.com   www.countrysideresidential.co.uk

The Countryside Group

The Countryside Group's two distinct brands, Countryside Residential and Copthorn Homes, are offering their customers a wider range of distinctive homes than ever before.

Countryside Residential offers its discerning purchasers new homes of character that reflect local building traditions. Their outstanding and individual appeal is combined with stunning interior layouts to create homes of distinction.

Their new homes also feature considerably more flexible living space with an ever increasing range of high quality features. Hand crafted kitchens are planned as the focal point of the home, usually with enough space in the larger homes for dining and relaxation.

Elegant bathrooms are much in evidence with most bedrooms having their own en-suite facilities. The ever expanding range of bespoke selections offered to purchase allows them to fully reflect their own tastes and ideas in their new home.

Countryside Residential continues to pride itself in creating new homes in the finest English tradition. Superb architectural detailing and a thorough understanding of local architectural styles is a feature of every Countryside home and the success of our approach is evidenced by the awards we receive.

RIBA Housing Design Awards for design excellence were recently awarded to St. Michaels Mead, Bishop's Stortford, Hertfordshire and the Fallowfield Village, Hallatrow, Somerset.

As with all Countryside developments, the architectural style of these award-winning schemes closely follows the local vernacular. At St Michaels Mead, The Village features a traditional Hertfordshire village street scene with Regents Square reflecting the grandeur of the Regency period with townhouses set around a classic square of magnificent proportions.

The Bishop's Stortford area is covered by Countryside's North Thames Region, who also have new homes available throughout Essex, with an exciting scheme planned for the future in the very centre of Cambridge.

Essex has always been at the heart of Countryside's development programme and it was here, at Great Notley Garden Village in Braintree, they were awarded the coveted 'What House?' Award for the Best Development in Britain.

Everything Countryside develop at Great Notley is eagerly awaited by discerning purchasers. The Stowe is the current development here featuring a range of delightful new homes from traditional almshouses to elegant homes with a distinctive 'county house' appeal.

Another Essex development is at Beaulieu Park, so aptly named by Henry VIII. Here Countryside has, once again, carefully recreated the local vernacular architecturally, with elevational detailing and designs taken from some of the country's finest homes.

Each part of Beaulieu Park has its own particular identity with features that reflect its particular design concept.

The other RIBA winner, Fallowfield Village, is being developed by Countryside's South West Region. Here the new homes reflect a traditional Somerset village, with a range of rendered homes set around a village green.

Another Somerset development is also arousing a great deal of interest, in Stoke Sub Hamdon on land formerly owned by the Duchy of Cornwall. The streetscape created finds its pattern from the historic village itself, drawing on local architectural elements for chimneys, windows, doors and dormers. Local Hamstone is used throughout and the roofshapes even include the use of traditional reed thatch.

Countryside South West is also achieving much in the Cotswolds, with sympathetic refurbishment of the old Estate cottages in Didmarton and a combined refurbishment and new build scheme in Burford.

In Cheltenham, Countryside is developing Wellington Place, 32 stunning apartments set behind an elegant Regency exterior that is being sympathetically restored to its former splendour. It has created a landmark building for this well known spa town with a great deal of interest shown from overseas purchasers as well as those in the UK.

Countryside's Northern Region is also enjoying a great deal of success, especially at Parr Woods where 31 prestigious homes are situated on part of Joseph Parr's original estate. Much of the woodland of mature oaks is being carefully preserved by Countryside as is the original stone wall. The new homes are all of magnificent proportions with stunning exterior elevations matched by interior layouts that feature an exceptionally high standard of finish and specification.

At the South Thames Region, Countryside's new homes also reflect their surroundings. Nevill Grange in Royal Tunbridge Wells, has prestigious character homes that have been created specially for their superb locations. Only 23 are available, each providing stylish, spacious and versatile living accommodation that has been carefully planned throughout.

At Kings Hill Villages in West Malling, Kent, Prince Regent Park will offer a stunning array of new homes from pretty gatehouses to impressive Regency style properties of magnificent proportions.

This new Village provides a uniquely rich and varied environment that Incorporates the very best features of village life with all the advantages of modern living. The new Countryside homes take advantage of their prestigious location here, with several properties adjoining the popular new Golf course.

Copthorn Homes, which specialises in stylish, affordable accommodation, has launched a new range of homes that truly respond to the way we live our lives today, with light, spacious interiors offering well planned and flexible living accommodation.

Copthorn Homes' goes from strength to strength, responding to our changing lifestyles by creating a range of homes that feel open and light filled, offering a generous amount of flexible living space. These are new homes where families can grow and evolve, and Copthorn's homes answer all their needs.

In many cases the roof space has been transformed into a fully integrated living space. It could be nursery, play room or teenagers' sitting room, or it could accommodate a home office, study or hobby room. Spacious kitchens have been designed to be the focus for family living. Some Copthorn homes even feature conservatories and master bedrooms which have the added benefit of a 'retreat' space for relaxing in at the end of the day.

Copthorn 'Choices and Options' Scheme allows customers to create the look they want, with a range of choices available at no extra cost and a range of cost effective options such as timber floors, bespoke kitchens and hand-painted bathroom tiles.

Copthorn have a range of superb homes throughout Essex, Hertfordshire and East London. Telephone Copthorn on 01277 262422 for further information.

marriage you might want to make provision for your children, otherwise the majority of your estate will go to your new spouse. It's best to do this through a solicitor. DIY packs are available but not recommended if you don't have legal training.

Should I Take Out Life Assurance?

The basic answer is yes. Life assurance will pay out to your spouse in the event of your death. This is essential if only one partner is the breadwinner, as a life assurance policy will help the surviving partner cover any debts like a mortgage that are left behind. The cheapest form of life assurance – term assurance – has recently become cheaper. It is one of the simplest financial products on the market.

You pay a small monthly premium and if you die your policy pays out an agreed lump sum – the sum assured. Most employers will offer life cover through an occupational pension fund, often at good rates, so do check this out as well. If you have taken out a life assurance policy with your mortgage lender it will only cover the cost of the mortgage. So, if you have any joint loans or outstanding payments it is a good safety net to take out life cover. This is especially true if only one spouse is the breadwinner or if you have children. Shop around before you sign up to a policy as age, sex and lifestyle all affect your premiums and companies offer different deals for each profile. It is important to get this right. Although premiums can be as low as £5 a month, you might be paying this over a period of 25 years. So it's important to find the best deal for you.

Should We Start a Joint Account?

For some people the idea of sharing an account is scarier than sharing your life and bed with someone. Opening a

We've a proposal to make.

The Persimmon
Homes Directory

Details of over 200 new home styles in 300 locations all over the UK

For your free Persimmon
New Homes Nationwide Directory,

please call **0645 10 10 11**, 7 days a week

Persimmon House, Fulford, York YO11 4EF

www.persimmon.plc.uk

PERSIMMON
Together, we make a home

Getting Married with Persimmon Homes

You've bought the rings, chosen the best man, booked the honeymoon...you've even managed to persuade your mother that your great aunt's grandchild, her husband and five children shouldn't be on the invitation list.

But there's one thing that isn't sorted out...you haven't yet found the home in which you will start your new life.

A recent survey by Britain's fourth-largest housebuilder, Persimmon Homes revealed that housebuyers felt that the best thing about moving house was that it represented a new beginning. And what better way to start your new life with the one you love than by moving house?

But do you really want to spend the months leading up to your wedding traipsing round estate agents and looking at a series of unsuitable properties? And do you want to spend the first few months of married life undoing someone else's decorating disasters?

So why not let Persimmon help you? Housebuyers say that the advantage of buying a new home is that you can create your own personality in a home that no-one has lived in before - and there will be fewer maintenance problems! After all, stripping wallpaper and painting windowsills are not how a newly-wed couple want to spend their evenings and weekends!

On top of the stresses and strains of organising a wedding, newlyweds certainly don't want hassle when it comes to moving house. Persimmon's Deputy Chairman Mike Allen appreciates this and aims to make the whole moving in process as easy as possible. He said: "Whatever home your buy from Persimmon and wherever you buy it, we really do aim to treat all our housebuyers with the care and respect they deserve - after all, this is probably going to be the largest single purchase they will ever make.

"Earlier this year we introduced the Persimmon Pledge - this nine-point charter means that housebuyers will receive the same quality of care wherever they are in the country and whatever home they buy.

"From the first day they take possession of their new Persimmon home, the company undertakes to make the settling-in period smooth and trouble-free as possible. And our Construction Clinic, held weekly outside normal office hours, means that couples won't need to take time off work if they need to see a Persimmon Construction Manager.

"We also ensure that we call in to see homebuyers within the first few days of occupation to make certain all is well with the new home.

"And just in case newly-weds find that they need a larger home as their family grows, buying their second Persimmon home will entitle them to a £500 discount against the price of their new property.

"Couples have so much to do when they marry - and we want to make the whole housebuying process painless so that they can enjoy married life to the full in their new home."

One of the best things about buying a new home is that it's fun! Your local newspaper will have details of the new developments in your area.

Many Persimmon showhomes are open in the evening and all are open at weekends, as well as during normal office hours, making viewing a new home convenient for everyone. The showhome will give you an idea of what your home could look like once you move in and on the financial side, talking to the sales negotiators will give you an indication of what financial arrangements are available on new properties - many developments offer part-exchange, special mortgage arrangements or other incentives (and showhomes are a great place to pick up interior design tips too!).

New homes come with NHBC guarantees as standard, and many come with security features such as window locks, security systems and smoke alarms - meaning that once you've moved in, you can just enjoy your life together and don't have to worry about fitting these features yourself and will have a greater peace of mind.

Persimmon Homes is the UK's fourth largest housebuilder and has been building houses for families and couples for over 25 years. What's unique about Persimmon is that they not only build a wide range of homes - from starter homes to luxury executive homes, from marina apartments to suburban family homes - but unlike many other developers don't duplicate the same house style across the country, which means that you're unlikely to see ëyour' house on another development in another part of the country!

Persimmon have 17 regional offices, and between them build at over 300 developments across the country.

So what is available from Persimmon? If you're London-based and looking for a stylish home, why not take a look at Persimmon's flagship Atlas Wharf apartments? Each apartment has stunning views of the Thames and a balcony or, in the case of the penthouses, a large terrace. The development will also incorporate a health club for the use of residents and secure parking facilities for all apartments. The one, two and three bedroom apartments are constructed in a single block of interlocking decadonal towers, based on an original concept by architect Sir Piers Goff, and prices range from £110,000 to £500,000.

Persimmon also builds a wide range of family homes in every part of the UK, from two and three bedroom semi-detached homes to luxury executive five bedroom houses.

The company also has properties for sale in the rural Yorkshire Dales as well as other stunning and peaceful parts of the UK - so if a rural idyll is your dream, Persimmon can help you find your ideal home.

Alternatively, if metropolitan living is more up your street, Persimmon has a wide range

Quality and style - a typical Persimmon home

of properties for couples and families alike in Britain's largest and most vibrant cities such as Manchester, Leeds and Glasgow.

When a couple start living together, they often have to overcome the challenges of geography - if each works in a different town or city, the problem arises of where to live. Who gets the longer drive to work? Whose family and friends need to be nearest?

The key to Persimmon's popularity with homebuyers is that although Persimmon takes pride in building in attractive locations - often with a real sense of seclusion or a rural feel - they are within easy reach of the main roads which link nearby towns and cities together.

Sometimes, a couple may be perfectly happy with the home in which they live, but want a holiday home to get away to at weekends. Persimmon's well-equipped seafront apartments with beautiful views, like those at Filey on the Yorkshire coast, or Port Solent on the south coast near Portsmouth, are an ideal getaway for couples who want to escape family and friends for a few days.

Mike Allen concluded: "Getting married is an exciting time for couples and we really do aim to help newly weds with every aspect of their house move.

"The great thing about buying a new house is that you can move in and start to live your life straight away - you don't have to worry about a thing."

joint account is often the easiest way to arrange your married finances. However, be aware that all debts are jointly owned. If you do set up a joint account, be honest about what you spend – it will avoid arguments. Some married couples prefer to keep an element of their finances separate to avoid feeling guilty when they want to splash out. It's a good idea to visit an independent financial adviser and discuss the best way to organize your money. Discuss setting up a savings account like an ISA or high-interest deposit account to start saving for the future.

What Happens to My Income Tax?

When you marry you are treated as individuals as far as your tax is concerned. However, until 6 April 2000, every couple is entitled to the married couple's allowance – a tax break. When you wed, make sure you ask the Inland Revenue for this tax relief. The husband receives this automatically but wives can claim half without their husband's knowledge. If the wife wants the whole tax break she will have to get his permission.

TIP: to make an election to give half or all of the married couple's allowance to your wife, you must make an election by notifying your tax office in writing. Ask for Form 18.

Capital Gains Tax – the transfer of assets will not be immediately taxed if a married couple is living together. Any gains made will be taxed when the object is sold.

Inheritance tax is not charged on gifts to your husband or wife before or after death.

What's the Best Way to Stay in the Black?

The most important thing is to be organized. Pay your bills on time to avoid incurring extra charges. If you have

The next best thing to one of our houses, is one of our houses.

Wherever we build our new homes ~ at dozens of developments throughout the Country ~ we know the importance of creating a real sense of community, with a wide variety of designs and careful attention to the landscape and the environment.

So when you choose an Alfred McAlpine home, you're sure of not just a beautiful house ~ but a beautiful place to live.

── WE ARE CURRENTLY BUILDING IN: ──

Cumbria, Dumfries & Galloway:
Tel: 01900 825351

Cleveland, County Durham, Northumberland, Tyne & Wear:
Tel: 0191 460 3000

Derbyshire, North Yorkshire, South Yorkshire, West Yorkshire:
Tel: 01924 201102

Cheshire, Lancashire, Merseyside:
Tel: 01925 830319 (24hr Answerphone Hotline)

Derbyshire, Leicestershire, Northamptonshire, Oxfordshire, Staffordshire, Warwickshire, West Midlands, Worcestershire:
Tel: 0121-746 3414 (24hr Answerphone Hotline)

Essex, Bedfordshire, Cambridgeshire, Hertfordshire, Kent, Suffolk:
Tel: 01992 560777 (24hr Answerphone Hotline)

Bristol, Gloucestershire, Newport, Rhondda, Somerset, Vale of Glamorgan, Wiltshire:
Tel: 01454 620202 (24hr Answerphone Hotline)

East Sussex, Hampshire, Surrey, West Sussex:
Tel: 01703 270043 (24hr Answerphone Hotline)

Alfred McAlpine Homes
RECOGNISED FOR QUALITY

Make your dream move into a brand new home

It is a well known fact that two of the most stressful events you can experience in life is organising a wedding and moving home. When you consider that the majority of couples who are planning to say 'I do' are also preparing to buy a new home together, it is easy to see how the stress levels can soar. However, if you are planning to buy a brand new home then you will discover that housebuilders are trying to take the stress and the strain out of moving.

Whether you are a first time buyer or are further up the property chain, you will discover that new housebuilders have a number of options which can be tailor made to suit your individual requirements. If you are a first time buyer and are paying rent, it can be extremely difficult to save up for your deposit. This is why Alfred McAlpine homes offers to pay the 5% deposit for first time buyers (subject to status) on selected plots at a number of

The two bedroom semi-detached housetype, which has proved very popular with first-time buyers.

the company's developments throughout the country. Other special offers can include fitted carpets, turfed gardens or electrical appliances such as a fridge freezer and washing machine.

If this is not your first home, selling your existing property can add to the hassle. There is the financial worry, waiting for the right offer, not to mention the misery and grief caused by being trapped within a housing chain. Most people know of someone who has experienced the strain of having a chain collapse just as they are about to move into their dream home. With the wedding day looming, this is one problem no one wants to have to face. To avoid the unnecessary, Alfred McAlpine Homes' part-exchange has, over the years, become a firm favourite with new home buyers. It bases its part-exchange offer on valuations carried out by two independent local firms. Offers are made, usually within 48 hours, subject to satisfactory survey, searches and proof of title. Once the offer has been accepted, you have no estate agent's fees to pay and you have the equivalent of a cash purchaser for your existing property.

Whatever your situation, you have peace of mind knowing that your brand new home is virtually mainte-

A typical Alfred McAlpine Homes street scene, incorporating the Elite Portfolio.

nance free, allowing you and your spouse to concentrate on the more pleasurable aspects of house buying. Early purchasers of a new home can work with the company to determine the interior design of their new home. As a general rule, the earlier the purchase is made, the more say you can have in the final look of your home, subject to general design restrictions. As part of the company's commitment to customer service, the sales negotiator will be on-hand to guide you through the specification options available on your new home. These may include a choice of colour schemes for the internal walls, the kitchen units and work-tops, kitchen appliances, the colour of the sanitary-ware and fitted kitchen furniture.

With the wedding and the house-moving blues now over, you and your bank balance will undoubtedly need a financial break. In a brand new home you don't have to live with other people's taste and spend time, money and effort getting rid of the avocado bathroom and the flowery wallpaper in the living room. A new home is like a blank canvas, on which you can create a style and atmosphere that suits your lifestyle and turns your new house into a real home for you both. Your new home will be finished to an excellent standard, so you may choose only to do the bare essentials

The four bedroom detached Sovereign design, part of the company's recently launched Elite Portfolio range.

like having carpets and curtains fitted. A new Alfred McAlpine home features a high standard of fixtures and fittings and comes complete with a 10 year NHBC guarantee.

It is comforting to know that new home buyers today are spoilt for choice and can benefit from a wealth of information, advice and expertise. Although buying a new house can be a little daunting don't let it get you down - it's just the beginning of a beautiful friendship!

For further information on Alfred McAlpine Homes and a list of developments in your area, please contact your regional office

Alfred McAlpine Homes Cumbria - 01900 825351

Alfred McAlpine Homes Northumbria - 0191 460 3000

Alfred McAlpine Homes Yorkshire Limited - 01924 201102

Alfred McAlpine Homes North West Limited - 01925 830319 (24hr Answerphone Hotline)

Alfred McAlpine Homes Midlands Limited - 0121 746 3414 (24hr Answerphone Hotline)

Alfred McAlpine Homes East Limited - 01992 560777 (24hr Answerphone Hotline)

Alfred McAlpine Homes South West Limited - 01454 620202 (24hr Answerphone Hotline)

Alfred McAlpine Homes Southern Limited - 01703 270043 (24hr Answerphone Hotline)

children, organize a monthly budget and try to stick to it as rigidly as you can. Keep a close eye on all financial matters. Try never to incur accidental charges from an unauthorized overdraft – these are astronomical. Borrowing money can be cheaper on a credit card in the short term or with a personal loan. Do check around for the best rates as APRs differ enormously. Any savings accounts should be watched rigorously to make sure the interest rate on the account does not drop – you can lose out.

What Happens to My Property?

In marriage, it doesn't matter who owns the property – you both have a claim to a share of it. The Matrimonial Causes Act 1973 gives guidelines as to how finance should be resolved. Usually, the judge will put the children first (if there are any), so the partner who stays with the children will keep the house. In Scotland the principle of 50:50 for matrimonial property remains, although 'matrimonial property' can be difficult to define; for example, the legal term doesn't include inheritance or gifts but joint gifts are included.

If you are taking out a joint mortgage, you are both responsible for keeping up the payments. For example, if one partner gets into trouble you could both be credit black-listed.

How Does Marriage Affect My Pension Plan?

Some women believe they can rely on their husband's pension. Schemes vary so you should check your entitlements. If a husband dies before his wife, the wife could get only a proportion of his entitlement. If a spouse marries again, the first spouse could end up with very little.

According to Richard Sax of the Solicitor's Family Law Association, proposed legislation on pension sharing should help. Courts currently have an obligation to consider pensions at the time of divorce. They have no power to split a pension between the parties. Since July 1996 courts can earmark part of the spouse's pension by ordering the pension provider to pay part of the death-in-service benefit lump sum or pension direct to the spouse. The pension-sharing bill will allow the court to divide the pension rights, including SERPS, between parties on divorce. The advantage of this is that there can be a clean split between parties. The proportion divided by the court will not be automatically 50:50. It could be anything or nothing. The Act will not be implemented until April 2000 at the earliest.

Since 17 May 1990 occupational pensions must offer equal benefits to men and women. So, if a woman dies before her husband, he will be entitled to the same benefits from her pension as a dependent wife would have been. Private pension schemes that are contracted out of SERPS must also offer equal benefits to both husbands and wives.

Benefits accruing from personal pension schemes not contracted to SERPS will depend on the individual contract.

Stress Busters

- Seek professional advice and organize your finances together.

- If you decide to have a joint account, be honest about what you have spent.

- Pay your bills on time to avoid incurring late payment penalties.

- Where kids are involved, organize a monthly budget and stick to it.

▌ Set up a savings account like an ISA or high-interest deposit account to prepare for your future life together.

▌ Take out life assurance.

▌ Keep informed of new financial products on the market and make sure you are getting the best deal for your mortgage and pension.

25 *Wedding Traditions*

Think of a wedding and images of rings, confetti, bridal veils and ritual are conjured up. But where do all these wedding traditions stem from? Have you ever wondered why a bride wears a veil or where the custom arose of carrying a bride over the threshold? Most of these quirky and much-loved traditions can be traced back to ancient and even more bizarre origins.

The Best Man

The best man's job is to protect the groom from any bad luck that might cross his path on the way to the church, especially something that might prevent the groom from getting to the church on time. When the best man pays a fee to the church minister, he should pay an odd amount to bring luck to the bride and groom.

The Bouquet

One of the most famous wedding customs occurs at the end of the reception. The bride throws her bouquet over her shoulder to the waiting clutches of any single women who desire to be next wed. If the groom removes the bride's garter and throws it over his shoulder, any unmarried man who catches it is supposed to be the next to marry.

The Bride Standing on the Left

This tradition has possible gruesome beginnings. Folklore suggests that the bride stood on the left during the marriage vows so her groom could hold on to her with his left arm, leaving his sword-arm free to fight off rivals.

The Bridesmaids Dressing Like the Bride

This comes from the ancient belief that the bride was under constant threat of evil spirits during the ceremony. The bridesmaids dressed like the bride to act as decoys to confuse the spirits.

Carrying Your Wife Over the Threshold

Strong husbands who carry their brides over the threshold may not realize they are harking back to an ancient superstition that tripping in the doorway would bring bad luck to the marriage. Any bow-legged grooms had better watch out, stoop too low and the evil spirits lurking in the threshold may leap onto your new wife's lap.

Days to Marry

Nowadays, the most popular day to marry is Saturday. This didn't used to be the case; an old rhyme advises against marrying towards the end of the week.

Monday for wealth
Tuesday for health
Wednesday for the best day of all
Thursday for losses
Friday for crosses
Saturday for no luck at all

Another rhyme advises against a May wedding:

Married when the year is new, he'll be loving, kind and true.
When February birds do mate, You wed nor dread your fate.
If you wed when March winds blow, joy and sorrow both you'll know.
Marry in April when you can, Joy for maiden and for Man.
Marry in the month of May, and you'll surely rue the day.
Marry when June roses grow, over land and sea you'll go.
Those who in July do wed, must labour for their daily bread.
Whoever wed in August be, many a change is sure to see.
Marry in September's shrine, your living will be rich and fine.
If in October you do marry, love will come but riches tarry.
If you wed in bleak November, only joys will come, remember.
When December snow falls fast, marry and true love will last.

In pagan times, May was considered an unlucky time to wed for several reasons. May was the time of the festival of Beltane. This festival was celebrated with outdoor orgies. Such a carnal free-for-all was seen as an inappropriate time to wed. In Roman times, May was the month of the Feast of the Dead and the festival of the Goddess of Chastity. Now this superstition has largely died out. In comparison, the summer was generally thought to be a fruitful time to marry, associated with the sun's fertility. In Scotland some brides would 'walk with the sun' to imbue themselves with the sun's powerful attributes. To do this the bride would walk from east to west on the south side of the church and continue walking around the church three times.

JASMINE

As a leader at the forefront of the bridal world, Jasmine has an extensive bridal wear range consisting of haute couture bridal gowns, adult bridesmaids dresses and elegant evening wear.

With over 100 different styles to choose from in a variety of 19 magnificent colours, the Jasmine bridesmaids and evening wear collection offers an enviable choice for any woman. As well, this collection is perfectly suited to registry office as well as civil wedding ceremonies.

Deciding from a selection of 250 wedding gowns has never been easy, but you need not worry. With Jasmine's expertly trained staff on hand to help you and give you the professional advice you require, you will be able to find the perfect wedding dress for that very special day. Keeping with the quality you would expect, all Jasmine bridal gowns are made to measure as not everybody has exactly the same 'standard' size.

With the vast amount of dresses designed by Jasmine it is impossible for us to make a brochure. So come to our central London showroom to view our collection. There is no need to make an appointment as our door is always open to you and we assure you of our best attention at all times.

21 GREAT TITCHFIELD STREET, LONDON W1P 7FD
TELEPHONE: 0207 636 6885

First Night

To encourage fertility, in Ireland, on the first night a laying hen would be tied to the bed. In Scotland, a lactating woman would prepare the newly weds' bed.

First Purchase

An old wives tale states that the partner who makes the first purchase after the wedding will be in the driving seat in the marriage. Some brides arrange to buy a trinket from their bridesmaid immediately after the ceremony to pip their new husbands to the post.

Flowers and Confetti

Flowers generally had protective associations with good health, good spirits and reflected the bride's bloom. In Victorian times individual flowers were used to exchange messages and each species had its own significance. A daisy meant innocence, a snowdrop hope, lemon blossom fidelity in love, cyclamen diffidence and hydrangea boastfulness. Throwing confetti over the ecstatic couple began as a pagan custom of showering the newly weds with grain to symbolize fruitfulness. Confetti is the Italian word for sweets and has a more recent origin in the Italian custom of throwing sweets over the bride and groom as they leave the church.

Journey to the Wedding

There are some old superstitions about the bride's journey to the church. Mirrors brought both good and bad luck. It was thought that if a bride looked in the mirror before she started her journey to the church it would bring her good luck. However, if she looked in the mirror having begun her journey it would bring bad luck to the marriage. And if the bride managed not to catch a glimpse of herself in the mirror, there were plenty of other random omens for the unfortunate bride to happen upon on her way to the church. Seeing an open grave, a monk, a nun, a pig or a lizard were all bad signs. On the other hand, good luck was denoted by the appearance of toads, spiders, lambs, black cats and rainbows.

Leap Year Proposals

Every leap year on 29 February it is customary for women to propose. This dates back to a time when this date was not recognized in English law. As a non-day, it was considered that customs and laws on 29 February had no meaning. Any woman who wanted to marry, but hadn't been proposed to, chose this day to ask the man of her choice.

Shoes

As well as 'just married' pinned on the bumper of the newly weds' car, shoes are sometimes seen to hold up the rear. This is a direct descendant of the Tudor practice of throwing shoes at newly weds. If the unfortunate bride or groom, or their carriage, collided with said shoes it was considered lucky. Some even weirder shoe customs have thankfully died out. One was for the groom to tap his bride on the head with his shoe to show who was boss (let's hope he used a clean shoe).

Something Old, Something New, Something Borrowed, Something Blue

This superstition dates back to a Victorian rhyme, although some of the superstitions mentioned are much older. The line continues *'Something old, Something new, Something borrowed, Something blue and a silver sixpence in your shoe.'* Traditionally 'something old' is the representation of the bride's maiden life, a link with her family heritage.

Often the bride wears a family heirloom, for example a piece of her grandmother's jewellery or even her dress. 'Something new' is for success and wealth in the bride's new life and can be anything new that the bride is wearing on her wedding day. 'Something borrowed' brings good luck to the couple. It is traditional to borrow an item that was worn at a happy marriage. This could be anything from a hankie to a garter. Wearing something blue is symbolic of purity and is thought to date back to the pre-mediaeval idea of blue representing purity. Finally, the 'silver sixpence' is no longer commonly used. The symbolic use of the sixpence was to represent financial and emotional wealth in the bride's life.

Surnames

It used to be considered bad luck for a woman to marry a man whose surname started with the same letter as hers.

Wedding Dress

Superstitions surround the bride's dress. It is thought to be unlucky for the bride to make it herself or for the dress to be fully complete before the ceremony. Some superstitious brides leave a stitch undone until their wedding day. A more common superstition is that the groom shouldn't see the bride's dress before the wedding.

As we all know, a white dress is the symbol of virginity. Before brides wore white dresses, they wore their best dress. A green dress was considered unlucky unless the bride was Irish. The expression 'a green gown' was used to refer to a loose woman whose dress was covered in grass stains due to rolling in the grass.

Married in White, you have chosen right,
Married in Blue, your love will always be true,
Married in Pearl, you will live in a whirl,
Married in Brown, you will live in a town,
Married in Red, you will wish yourself dead,
Married in Yellow, ashamed of your fellow,
Married in Green, ashamed to be seen,
Married in Pink, your spirit will sink,
Married in Grey, you will go far away,
Married in Black, you will wish yourself back.

Wedding Rings on the Third Finger

The position of wedding rings on the third finger of the left hand could be a modern offshoot of the Egyptian idea of the 'vena amoris', a throbbing love vein thought to connect the third finger with the heart.

The Wedding Veil

The wedding veil was perhaps originally worn by Roman brides and was used to dispel evil spirits intent on leeching on to the bride during the ceremony. It is also believed to have derived from the practice of throwing a blanket over the bride's head while she was being kidnapped by her over-eager husband-to-be. Another theory is that it was used for a more practical reason, to prevent potential husbands from running scared if the blushing bride was less than charming.

26 *On the Day Check-list*

Health and Beauty

▌ Ask someone to call you or wake you up so you don't panic about over-sleeping.

▌ Get up in good time – not too early, you want to look your best.

▌ Eat a gorgeous healthy breakfast (see page 206).

▌ Put on a stimulating face mask to make your skin glow – make sure it's one you've used before and know you're not allergic to.

▌ Have a relaxing bath.

▌ Apply body and face moisturiser and wait for them to dry.

▌ Before you dress you could do some relaxation exercises, perhaps some deep breathing or meditation. If you can afford it, hire a professional masseur to give you some gentle pressure point therapy like reflexology.

Bride

▌ Add the finishing touches to your hair.

▌ Apply make-up carefully.

▌ Add the finishing touches to your nails – wait for them to dry.

▌ Put on your dress. (If your dress goes over your head, put it on first and place a clean towel around the front of your dress before you do your hair or make-up to avoid stains.)

▌ When you are completely ready, put on your headdress, jewellery and/or veil.

▌ If you're superstitious don't forget to wear something old, new, borrowed and blue.

Possible Wedding Breakfast

▌ Earl Grey or herbal tea – steer clear of coffee unless you're a total addict. Too much caffeine could add to your wedding jitters.

▌ A bowl of muesli – full of energy to stop you fainting at the altar.

▌ Wholemeal toast and jam.

▌ Orange juice.

▌ A boiled egg (if you're still hungry).

Nothing too fattening to avoid putting any strain on your perfectly fitting wedding clothes!

Groom

▌ Style your hair.

▌ If you have a few spots on the day, you could cheat and use some light spot cover. Do this only if you have practised before the day and before you are dressed.

▌ If you decide to polish your shoes on the day, do this before you are dressed as shoe polish is impossible to get off clothes.

▌ Dress in your wedding outfit.

As a final calmer, have a glass of champagne before you take the big step and remember to enjoy your day. It will probably be the most wonderful day of your life.

Index

Index of Advertisers

The Lifeplanner Series

The Lifeplanner series addresses personal finance and consumer issues in a jargon-free, readable way, taking the fear out of planning your life. So whether you are thinking about buying a house, having a baby, getting married or planning your retirement the Lifeplanner series will help you do so wisely.

Titles available are:

Balancing Your Career, Family and Life
Getting Married
Landing Your First Job
Making the Most of Being a Student
Making the Most of Retirement
The Young Professional's Guide to Personal Finance
Your Child's Education
Your First Home: A Practical Guide to Buying and Renting
Your First Investment Portfolio

Available from all good booksellers. For further information on the series, please contact:

Kogan Page
120 Pentonville Road
London
N1 9JN
Tel: 0171 278 0433
Fax: 0171 837 6348
e-mail: kpinfo@kogan-page.co.uk
or visit our website: www.kogan-page.co.uk